PRINCE2® 6th Edition

Other publications by Van Haren Publishing

Van Haren Publishing (VHP) specializes in titles on Best Practices, methods and standards within four domains:

- IT and IT Management
- Architecture (Enterprise and IT)
- Business Management and
- Project Management

Van Haren Publishing is also publishing on behalf of leading organizations and companies: ASLBiSL Foundation, BRMI, CA, Centre Henri Tudor, Gaming Works, IACCM, IAOP, IFDC, Innovation Value Institute, IPMA-NL, ITSqc, NAF, KNVI, PMI-NL, PON, The Open Group, The SOX Institute.

Topics are (per domain):

IT and IT Management
ABC of ICT
ASL®
CATS CM®
CMMI®
COBIT®
e-CF
ISO/IEC 20000
ISO/IEC 27001/27002
ISPL
IT4IT®
IT-CMF™
IT Service CMM
ITIL®
MOF
MSF
SABSA
SAF
SIAM™
TRIM
VeriSM™

Enterprise Architecture
ArchiMate®
GEA®
Novius Architectuur Methode
TOGAF®

Business Management
BABOK® Guide
BiSL® and BiSL® Next
BRMBOK™
BTF
EFQM
eSCM
IACCM
ISA-95
ISO 9000/9001
OPBOK
SixSigma
SOX
SqEME®

Project Management
A4-Projectmanagement
DSDM/Atern
ICB / NCB
ISO 21500
MINCE®
M_o_R®
MSP®
P3O®
PMBOK® Guide
PRINCE2®

For the latest information on VHP publications, visit our website: www.vanharen.net.

PRINCE2®
6th Edition
A Pocket Guide

Bert Hedeman
Ron Seegers

Colophon

Title:	PRINCE2® 6th Edition – A Pocket Guide
Series:	Best Practice
Authors:	Bert Hedeman (HWP Consulting), Ron Seegers (Projectmeester)
Reviewers:	Marc Kouwenhoven (nThen!) Jaap Germans (Pinkelephant) Henny Portman (HWP Consulting) Georges Kemmerling (Quint Wellington Redwood)
Final Editor:	Bert Hedeman
Text editor:	Carmen Tjin
Publisher:	Van Haren Publishing, Zaltbommel, www.vanharen.net
ISBN Hard copy:	978 94 018 0579 7
ISBN EBook pdf:	978 94 018 0581 0
ISBN EPub	978 94 018 0583 4
Print:	First edition, first impression, September 2009 Second edition, first impression, April 2018 Third edition, first impression, June 2018 Fourth edition, first impression, February 2020
Layout and type setting:	S&B IT Services, Amersfoort – NL
Copyright:	© Van Haren Publishing, 2018

Contents

PART I INTRODUCTION

Chapter 1
Introduction

PRINCE2® is a generic project management method which focuses on the management aspects of projects. PRINCE2® was originally launched in 1996 by the CCTA. Since then several versions have been launched. The latest update of the method has been published in 2017.

PRINCE2® is now a registered trade mark of AXELOS. Additionally AXELOS provides certification to organizations, activities and persons related (but not limited to) projects, programmes and risk based on the methods owned by AXELOS, such as ITIL®, PRINCE2 Agile™, MSP™, P3O™, MoP™, M_o_R® and P3M3™.

1.1 The purpose of this guide

This pocket guide supplies a summary of the PRINCE2 method. It is intended to provide a quick introduction as well as a structured overview of the method and to act as a reference for those who have studied the method in the past and want to use the method now in the day-to-day management of their projects.

1.2 What is a project?

A project is a set of related activities within a temporary organization that is created to deliver, according to agreed conditions, one or more predefined products or services. Within the context of the method of PRINCE2 a project is defined as:

> A temporary organization that is created for the purpose of delivering one or more business products according to an agreed business case.

1.3 Why are projects important?

Projects are carried out mainly when the work cannot be carried out properly with normal business operations. One of these conditions is when the business operations have to transform to meet new requirements, in order to survive or to compete in the future.

The temporary organization of projects makes it possible to unite all stakeholders to deliver the required products or services. The structure and processes within a proper project management method enforce focus, support and commitment for the products and services that are to be delivered. Projects are therefore an important means to supporting change.

As business change is becoming more and more important in business operations as well as in the public domain, projects nowadays are crucial in professional life.

1.4 Projects versus business as usual

Based on the definition of a project, there are a number of characteristics of projects that distinguish project work from regular business operations:

- **Change** – Most projects are carried out in a changing environment and are, at the same time, the means by which the organization introduces these changes. This will often cause severe resistance from the parties involved. The project has to manage this resistance and, increasingly, has to contribute in diminishing this resistance in addition to its requirements to deliver the predefined products and services.
- **Temporary** – This is an essential condition for a project. Without this, there is no project. A project ends automatically when the predefined products or services are handed over to the customer. Projects by nature are finite, they have a predefined start and end.
- **Cross-functional** – Projects involve a team of people with different skills and functions, most often from different organizational entities. This can be from within a single organization or from several organizations.
- **Unique** – Every project is different, even when an identical product or service is delivered. The context is always different and there are always differences in objectives, new team members or other parties involved. This makes each project unique in relation to every other project.
- **Uncertainty** – All the characteristics above result in uncertainty and this will always result in opportunities and threats. You cannot exclude this, you can only manage it. Projects are typically more risky than the normal business operations. Management of risk (uncertainty) is therefore a core focus of project management.

1.5 What is project management?

Project management is the planning, delegating, monitoring and control of all aspects of the project, and the motivation of those involved, to achieve the project objectives within the expected performance targets for time, cost, quality, scope, risks and benefits, see figure 1.1.

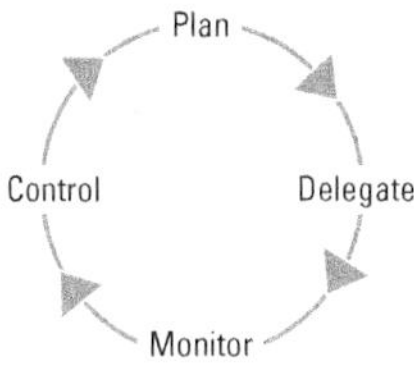

Figure 1.1 Project management cycle (Source: AXELOS)

The purpose of project management is to retain control over the specialist work required to create the project's products (products and services).

Project management, therefore, within this definition is not limited to the work of the project manager. Project management is a duty of all involved in the management of the project. This includes the executive, the other members of the project board, the project manager, the project support and the respective team managers.

1.6 What does a project manager do?

The project manager is responsible for the day-to-day management of the project, within the directions set by the executive/project board.

As part of this day-to-day management, the project manager is responsible for the planning, delegation, monitoring and control of the work to be carried out, as well as for the management of other aspects of the project, such as:

- Engagement of stakeholders to create support and commitment and to diminish resistance;
- Motivation of team members and all who are contributing to the project.

1.7 What is it all parties involved wish to control?

There are considered to be six basic aspects involved in any project:

- **Costs** – the costs involved to create the defined project products. This also includes the costs to manage the project.
- **Time** – the total lifecycle of the project and/or the date of handing over the project product.

- **Quality** – the product's ability to meet its requirements.
- **Scope** – what is included in the project works? What has to be delivered and what not? What work has to be carried out and what not?
- **Risks** – the management of threats as well as the management of the opportunities.
- **Benefits** – the benefits to be realized based on the project product.

PRINCE2 defines the project product as that which the project must deliver to be accepted. Project products are all products to be created during the project lifecycle including the management products.

In addition to these basic aspects, other aspects are often involved in projects, such as health, environment, safety and security. These aspects can be controlled as part of the quality aspect.

Chapter 2
Introduction to PRINCE2

PRINCE2 is a structured project management method, based on best practice.

PRINCE2 is a non-proprietary method. Project managers and others are free to use the method in their own practice.

PRINCE2 is truly generic. It can be applied to any project, regardless of scale, type, organization, geography or culture. However the method always has to be tailored to the project at hand.

PRINCE2 achieves this by isolating the management aspects of project work from the specialist contributions, such as design, construction, etc. However the specialist work can easily be integrated with the PRINCE2 method.

Because PRINCE2 is generic and based on proven principles, organizations can easily adopt the method as a standard and tailor it to their own organization and substantially improve their organizational capability to perform projects and deliver change.

PRINCE2 is protected by trademark. Professional training is restricted to Accredited Training Organizations and their Affiliates. See the Axelos website (www.axelos.com).

2.1 Structure of PRINCE2

The PRINCE2 method addresses project management from four different perspectives:

- **Principles** – are the guiding obligations of good practices which determine whether the project is genuinely being managed using PRINCE2.
- **Themes** – describe the aspects of project management that must be addressed continually and in parallel throughout the project. The themes explain the specific treatment required by PRINCE2 for various project management disciplines and why they are necessary.
- **Processes** – describe a step-wise progression through the project lifecycle. Each process provides checklists of recommended activities, products and related responsibilities.
- **Project environment** – relates to the tailoring of PRINCE2 to the specific context of the project. This context depends on specific project factors as well as environmental factors.

2.2 What makes a project a PRINCE2 project?

A project is considered a PRINCE2 project if at a minimum it applies:

- All seven PRINCE2 principles;
- The minimum requirements specified in the PRINCE2 themes;
- Processes that comply with the purpose and objectives of the PRINCE2 processes;
- All techniques recommended by PRINCE2 or equivalent alternative techniques.

2.3 What PRINCE2 does not provide

There are three broad areas which are deliberately left outside the scope of PRINCE2:

- **Specialist work** – PRINCE2's strength is in its wide application. Consequently industry-specific or type-specific activities are not within the scope of PRINCE2. However PRINCE2 can easily be aligned to specialist lifecycle models.
- **Techniques** – There are many proven planning and control techniques. Such techniques are well documented elsewhere. Techniques are only included in PRINCE2 when they contribute to the specific PRINCE2 treatment of a theme, e.g. the quality review technique in the quality theme.
- **Leadership capability** – Leadership and other social skills are inherently important in project management but impossible to codify in a method. Also these are well documented elsewhere. However the principles, themes and processes of PRINCE2 facilitate a good performance of these skills and thus contribute to the performance of the project too.

2.4 Customer/supplier environment

PRINCE2 is based on a customer/supplier environment. The customer is the person or group who commissioned the work and who will benefit from the project's products. A supplier is a person or group who is responsible for the delivery of (a part of) the project's products. In a project there may be several suppliers organizations.

Customers and suppliers can be part of the same organization. They can also be part of different organizations. Within the customer we can again recognize users and business representatives.

In commercial projects with different organizations, such as external suppliers, each organization may have its own business cases, management systems, governance, delivery approaches and corporate cultures.

A project can be a stand-alone project or a part of a programme or portfolio. PRINCE2 refers to the organization that commissions a project as the corporate, programme management or customer.

2.5 Benefits of PRINCE2

PRINCE2 delivers benefits to all parties concerned, especially the customers, suppliers and the project manager:

- Proven best practice, widely recognized;
- Can be applied to any type of project;
- Provides a common vocabulary and approach;
- Integrates easily with industry-specific standards;

- Allocates resources as part of the go/no-go moments;
- Thorough but economical structure of reports;
- Restricts meetings to only those that are essential;

- Promotes learning and continuous improvement;
- Promotes reuse of project assets, facilitates staff mobility;
- Availability of Accredited Training Organizations;

- Clear roles and responsibilities for all participants;
- Focus on continuous justification of the project;
- Participation of stakeholders in planning and decision making;
- Management by exception for all levels of the project;

- Product focus: what a project will deliver;
- Plans meet the needs of different levels of management;
- Quality control during whole lifecycle of the project;
- Manages business and project risks;
- Ensures relevant issues are escalated;
- Diagnostic tool for assurance and assessments.

Chapter 3
Principles

The purpose of PRINCE2 is to provide a project management method that can be applied regardless of project scale, type, complexity and culture, and irrespective of the environmental factors.

This is possible because PRINCE2 is principle-based. Principles are characterized as universal, self-validating and empowering.

3.1 Continued business justification

A requirement for each PRINCE2 project is that:
- There is a justifiable reason to start it;
- The justification may change, but should remain valid throughout the life span of the project;
- The justification is documented and approved.

The justification drives the decision-making process. In PRINCE2 the justification is documented in a business case. Even projects that are compulsory require justification to validate the option chosen to comply with the compulsive requirement.

3.2 Learn from experience

In PRINCE2 the project and management approaches are perfected through learning from experience:
- When starting the project, lessons from previous projects should be reviewed to see if these lessons could be applied;
- As the project progresses, lessons should be included in all reports and reviews. The goal is to seek opportunities to implement improvements during the project lifecycle;
- As the end of the intermediate stages and as the project closes, the project should pass the lessons on to the relevant corporate, programme management or customer.

It is everyone's responsibility to continuously seek lessons rather than waiting for someone else to provide them.

3.3 Defined roles and responsibilities

A PRINCE2 project has defined and agreed roles and responsibilities, with an organizational structure that reflects the stakeholder interests of the business, user and supplier:

- Business sponsors endorse the objectives and should ensure the business investment provides value for money;
- Users who, after the project is completed, will use the project's products to enable the organization to gain the expected benefits;
- Suppliers will provide the resources required by the project.

Therefore all three stakeholder interests need to be represented effectively in the project organization, at the delivery level as well as at the directing level.

3.4 Manage by stages

A PRINCE2 project is planned, monitored and controlled on a stage-by-stage basis.

Management stages provide senior management with control at major decision points by having a high level project plan for the total project and a detailed stage plan for the next stage. At the end of each intermediate stage, the next stage plan will be produced and the project plan will be updated.

PRINCE2 requires a minimum of two management stages: one initiation stage and one or more delivery stages.

3.5 Manage by exception

A PRINCE2 project has defined tolerances for each project objective to establish limits of delegating authority.

PRINCE2 enables appropriate governance by defining a distinct responsibility and accountability at each level of the project by:

- Delegating authority so that tolerances are set against the objectives (time, cost, quality, scope, risk and benefits) for each level of plan;
- Establishing controls so that if those tolerances are forecast to be exceeded they are immediately referred up to the next management level for a decision on how to proceed;

- Establishing an assurance mechanism so that each management level can be confident that such controls are effective.

Management by exception provides the effective use of senior management time and reduces the time-consuming meetings that projects are normally burdened with.

3.6 Focus on products

A PRINCE2 projects focuses on the definition and delivery of products, in particular their quality criteria.

A successful project is output-oriented, not activity-oriented. An output-oriented project is one that agrees and defines the project's products including the quality requirements and acceptance criteria prior to undertaking the activities required to produce them. The set of agreed products defines the scope of a project and provides the basis for planning and control.

Without a product focus, projects are exposed to several major risks such as acceptance disputes, scope-creep, user dissatisfaction and under-estimation of acceptance activities.

3.7 Tailor to suit the project environment

PRINCE2 is tailored to suit the project's environment, size, complexity, importance, capability and risk:

- Processes can be combined or adapted;
- Themes can be applied using techniques appropriate to the project;
- Roles can be combined or split;
- Management products can be adapted, combined or split;
- Terminology can be aligned to organizational standards.

The project manager is responsible for tailoring the project to suit the project environment. The tailoring must be approved by the project board.

To ensure that all people involved understand how the method is being tailored, the tailoring should be documented in the PID for that particular project.

PART II THEMES

Chapter 4
Introduction to PRINCE2 themes

The PRINCE2 themes describe the aspects of project management that must be addressed continually and integrally throughout the project, see figure 4.1:

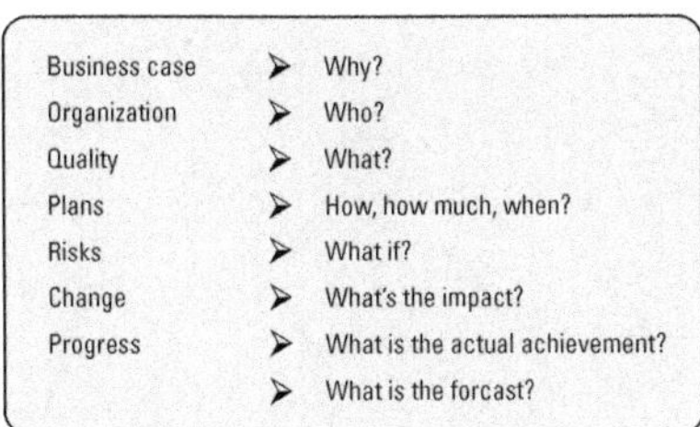

Figure 4.1 The PRINCE2 themes

- **Business case theme** – describes how the idea is developed into a viable investment proposition for the organization and how project management maintains the focus on the organization's objectives throughout the project.
- **Organization theme** – describes the roles and responsibilities in the temporary project organization that are required to manage the project effectively.
- **Quality theme** – describes how the original outline is developed into the quality criteria and how project management ensures that these criteria are subsequently delivered.
- **Plans theme** – describes the steps required to develop plans and suggests the product-based planning approach to be applied.
- **Risk theme** – describes how project management manages the uncertainties in plans and in the wider project environment.
- **Change theme** – describes how project management assesses and acts upon issues which have a potential impact on any of the baseline aspects of the project. Issues may be unanticipated problems or concerns, requests for change, or instances of quality failure.
- **Progress theme** – addresses the ongoing viability of the plans. This then explains the decision-making process for approving plans, the monitoring of the actual performance, the corrective actions to be taken and the escalation process if the performance is forecast to exceed the agreed tolerances.

All seven themes must be applied throughout the project, but should be tailored to fit the project context.

Chapter 5
Business case

5.1 Purpose of the business case theme

The purpose of the business case theme is to establish mechanisms to judge whether the project is and remains desirable, viable and achievable, as a means to support the decision making in relation to its investment.

5.2 Business case defined

The key concepts related to the business justification are:

- **Output** – any of the project's products (whether tangible or intangible) that is handed over to the users;
- **Outcome** – the result of the change derived from using these outputs, normally affecting real-world behaviour and/or circumstances;
- **Benefit** – the measurable improvement resulting from an outcome that is perceived as an achievement by one or more stakeholders;
- **Dis-benefit** – a measurable decline resulting from an outcome perceived as negative by one or more stakeholders, which reduces one or more organizational objectives.

The senior user is responsible for specifying the benefits and dis-benefits and subsequently for realizing the benefits and minimalizing the dis-benefits resulting from the use of the project outputs. The executive owns the business case and is responsible for the project alignment with the corporate, programme or customer objectives and realizes value for money.

Some projects may be justified by return on investment; others may be justified by non-financial benefits. Even compulsory projects will need business justification. These projects need to be judged on how the (compulsory) requirements should be met (gold, silver or bronze).

5.3 PRINCE2 requirements for the business case theme

A PRINCE2 project must, at a minimum:

- Define and maintain a business case;
- Define and maintain the benefits management approach;
- Define and document the roles and responsibilities related to the business case and the benefits management approach.

The purpose of the business case is to document the business justification. The purpose of the benefits management approach is to document the benefits management actions and benefits reviews that are needed to ensure that the project's outcomes are achieved and to confirm that the project's benefits are realized.

5.4 PRINCE2 approach to the business case theme

The outline business case is developed at the start of up the project (or even before), further detailed during the initiation the project and maintained throughout the life of the project. The business case is being formally verified by the project board at each key decision point, so that it can be confirmed throughout the project lifecycle that the project is still desirable, viable and achievable.

Alongside the business case, the benefits management approach is developed, maintained and verified. The updated business case and benefits management approach are the basis for the benefits reviews during the project lifecycle and the post-project, see figure 5.1.

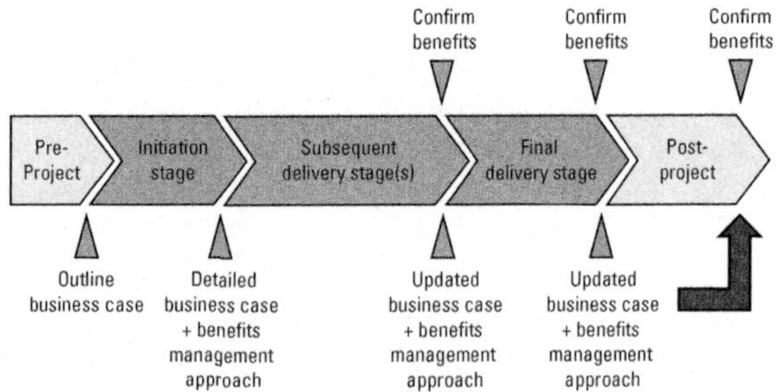

Figure 5.1 Development path business case theme (based on: AXELOS Ltd.)

5.4.1 Developing the business case

The executive owns the business case. However he can delegate the development of the business case to a business analyst or to the project manager. Project assurance may assist with the development of the business case.

The outline business case is developed in starting up a project and integrated in the project brief. The outline business case may be derived from the project mandate. During initiating a project, the detailed business case is developed and integrated in the project initiation documentation (PID).

5.4.2 Reviewing and verifying the business case

The business case is reviewed and verified by the project manager:

- As part of the impact assessment of any new or revised issue or risk;
- At the end of each management stage to determine if an update is needed;
- During the final management stage to assess the project's performance and the likelihood that the outcomes will provide the expected benefits.

The business case is reviewed and verified by the project board:

- At the end of starting up a project to authorize the project initiation;
- At the end of initiating a project to authorize the project;
- As part of the approval of the exception plan to authorize the revised stage and the continuation of the project;
- At the end of each management stage to authorize the next stage and the continuation of the project;
- At the closure of the project by the project board to verify an accurate basis for the benefits review to be carried out.

The business case is reviewed and verified by the corporate, programme management or customer as part of the benefits reviews after closure of the project to determine if the expected benefits are realized.

It is the responsibility of the executive to assure the other project stakeholders that the project remains desirable, viable and achievable at all times.

5.4.3 Ensuring and confirming that the benefits are realized

The approach to confirm the benefits is to:

- Identify the benefits and who is responsible for realizing these benefits;
- Select objective measures that reliably prove the benefits;
- Collect the baseline measures;
- Decide how, when and by whom the benefits measures will be collected.

The senior user is responsible for specifying the benefits and is held to account by the executive that the expected benefits are realized.

The benefits management approach is first created in the initiation stage and updated during the subsequent stage boundaries, and is finally updated at closing of a project by the project manager.

Benefits realized during the execution of the project should be confirmed by the senior user and included in the end stage and closure reports by the project manager.

The executive is responsible for assuring that the benefits reviews are held. After closure of the project this responsibility is transferred to corporate, programme management or customer.

5.5 Content of a business case

The business case should include the following:

- Executive summary;
- Reasons: why this project is needed and how the project will support the corporate strategies and objectives;
- Business options and why these options were not selected. The 'do nothing' option should always be referred to. All other options should be compared with the 'do nothing' option;
- Expected benefits and dis-benefits: whether financial or non-financial. All benefits should be aligned with corporate objectives and strategies, mapped from the outputs provided by the project, quantified, measurable and owned. Set a benefit tolerance for each benefit;
- Timescale: the period during which the project costs will be incurred and the period upon which the cost/benefits analysis will be based;

- Costs: derived from the project plan together with the assumptions upon which they are based, including the ongoing operational and maintenance costs and the funding arrangements;
- Major risks: summary of the aggregated risks and a highlight of the major risks;
- Investment appraisal: assessment of the development, operational and maintenance costs against the value of the benefits.

5.6 Guidance for effective business case management

Small projects – In small projects there is no separate business case. The business case is just a section of the project initiation documentation (PID).

Commercial projects – An external supplier has its own business case mostly directly focused on the profit to be realized with the execution of the project. However the business case of the customer is referred to as the business case of the project.

Projects in a programme – The project business case is derived from the programme business case but documenting it for the project cannot be skipped. The benefits management approach can be created and maintained by the programme management. The project benefits reviews can be included in the programme benefit reviews.

Agile projects – Products are implemented incrementally and benefits reviews should therefore already be carried out during as well as after the project. In the business case often the best, expected and worst case of the products to be delivered are shown, given a fixed cost, time and quality.

5.7 Techniques: investment appraisal

Methods often applied to investment appraisals are:

- Return on investment: profit as a percentage of the initial investment;
- Net present value: discounted future cash flows minus the initial investment;
- Break-even point: number of products needed to recover the initial investment;
- Payback period: the period needed to recover the initial investment.

5.8 Responsibilities business case theme

For the responsibilities of the business case theme, see table 5.1.

Table 5.1 Roles and responsibilities of the business case theme

Corporate, programme management or customer (CPMC)	Project manager (PM)
• Provide mandate and standards to which the business case (BC) needs to be developed • Hold senior user to account for realizing the benefits (post-projects) • Accountable for benefits management approach (post-project)	• Prepare the BC on behalf of the executive • Conduct impact analyses on issues and risks that may affect project's viability • Assess and update the BC at the end of each management stage • Assess and report on project performance at project closure
Executive • Own business case for duration of project • Approve benefits management approach • Ensure alignment with business strategies • Secure funding **Senior user** • Specify the benefits in the BC • Ensure desired project outcome is specified • Ensure that project produces products which deliver the desired outcomes • Ensure the expected benefits are realized • Provide actual versus forecast benefits statement at benefits reviews	**Project assurance** • Assist in development of the BC • Ensure viability BC is constantly reassessed • Monitor changes to the project plan to identify any impact on the BC • Verify and monitor BC against issues and progress • Review impact assessments on project plan and BC • Monitor project finance on behalf of CPMC • Ensure project stays aligned with CPMC strategies • Verify and monitor that the benefits management approach aligns with CPMC
Senior supplier • Approve supplier's BC (if any) • Confirm that the products required can be delivered within expected costs and time	**Project support** • Keep the BC under configuration • Advice PM about changes that may affect the BC

Chapter 6
Organization

6.1 Purpose of the organization theme

The purpose of the organization theme is to define and establish the project's structure of accountability and responsibilities.

A successful project management team should:

- Have business, user and supplier representation;
- Ensure appropriate governance by defining responsibilities for directing, managing and delivering the project;
- Have an effective approach to engage the stakeholders;
- Review project roles throughout the project to ensure the continuous effectiveness of the team.

A stakeholder is any individual, group or organization that can affect, can be affected by, or perceive itself to be affected by, an initiative.

6.2 Organization defined

PRINCE2 states that a project always has three primary categories of stakeholders and that their interests must be satisfied in the project if the project is to be successful. In order to realize this it is necessary to have business, user and supplier representation at the management level of the project, see figure 6.1:

- **Business** – are those who have to justify the investment in the project. The project should provide them value for money;
- **Users** – are those who will use, operate, maintain or support the project's output, or will be affected by the output;.
- **Suppliers** – are those who will provide the necessary resources and skills and deliver the project's output.

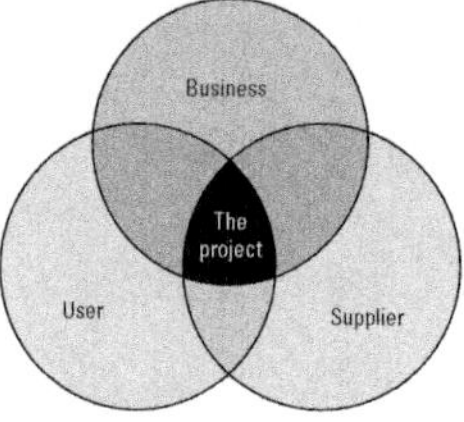

Figure 6.1 The three project interests (source: AXELOS Ltd.)

6.3 Levels of organization

The project management structure consists of four levels, three within the project, forming the project management team and the corporate, programme management or customer, outside the project, see figure 6.2.

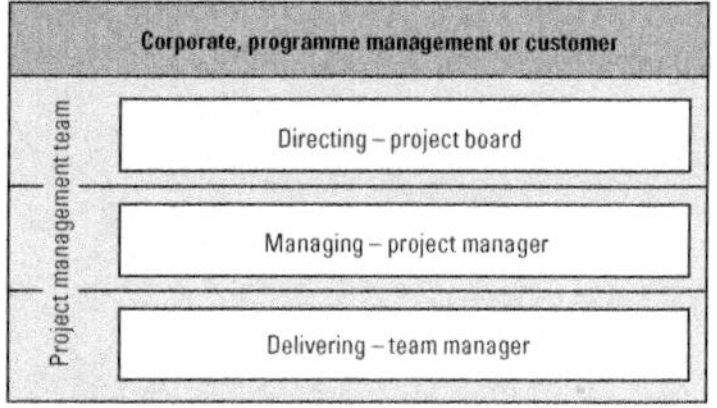

Figure 6.2 Levels of management (source: AXELOS Ltd.)

- **Corporate, programme management or customer** – This level is not part of the project, but is responsible for commissioning and overall direction of the project within the strategy of the corporate, programme management or customer;
- **Directing** – The project board is responsible for the overall direction and management of the project within the constraints set out by corporate, programme management or customer;
- **Managing** – The project manager is responsible for the day-to-day management of the projects within the constraints set out by the project board;
- **Delivering** – The team manager is responsible for the daily management of the individual work packages and for the delivery of the project output within the defined objectives.

The project organization consists of the project management team and the team members. The team members are responsible for the actual realization of the project's products.

6.4 PRINCE2 requirements for the organisation theme

A PRINCE2 project must, at a minimum:

- Define and maintain the organization structure and roles;
- Define and maintain the rules for delegating change authority;
- Define and maintain the communication management approach.

The purpose of the communication management approach is to describe the means and frequency of communication with the project stakeholders to facilitate the engagement of these stakeholders with the project.

The organizational structure and roles, the rules for delegating the change authority and the communication management approach should all be documented in the project initiation documentation (PID).

6.5 Project management team

The project management team consists of the project board, the project manager, the team managers, the project assurance, the change authority and the project support, see figure 6.3.

Project board – is the highest management platform of the project. The board should always represent the business, user and supplier interests. This is usually done through the executive, senior user and senior supplier. The project board is accountable for the success of the project.

The responsibilities of the project board are:

- Being accountable for the success of the project;
- Providing unified direction and guidance to the project;
- Delegating day-to-day management effectively to the project manager;
- Facilitating the integration with the functional units;
- Providing funding and the resources required;
- Ensuring effective decision making;
- Providing visible and sustained support to the project manager;
- Ensuring effective communication with all stakeholders.

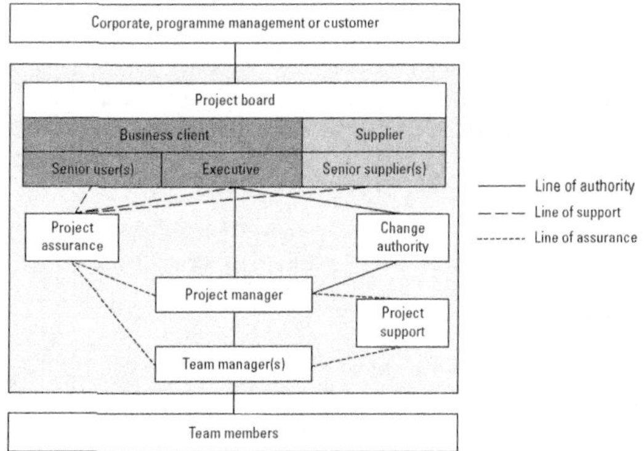

Figure 6.3 Project management team (based on: AXELOS Ltd.)

Members of the project board should have authority and credibility, should be able to delegate and should be available.

Executive – is chairman of the project board, and ultimately accountable for the success of the project and the key decision maker. In this respect the project board is not a democratic entity, but a management platform for decision making. The executive is responsible for the continuous viability of the project from the customer's point of view. There is only one executive.

Senior user – represents the interests of the users on the board. The senior user is responsible for specifying the needs of the users, reviewing the project's products from the users' point of view, making available the necessary user resources and communicating about the project with other user representatives. The senior user is further responsible for specifying the benefits and is held to account by demonstrating to corporate, programme management or customer that the forecast benefits have been realized. This role can be fulfilled by more than one person.

Senior supplier – represents the interests of the suppliers on the board. The senior supplier is accountable for the (quality of the) products delivered by the suppliers within time and budget agreed. Within this role, he is responsible for providing the suppliers' resources to the project, and ensuring that the design and realization are feasible and realistic. This role can be fulfilled by more than one person.

In most cases the senior supplier also represents the interests of those who will maintain the project output after closure.

The project board needs to represent all interested parties. Therefore several senior users and suppliers can be appointed. In case, however, that the project board becomes too large, it is then advisable to install separate user and supplier boards who will be represented on the project board by a senior user or senior supplier, see figure 6.4.

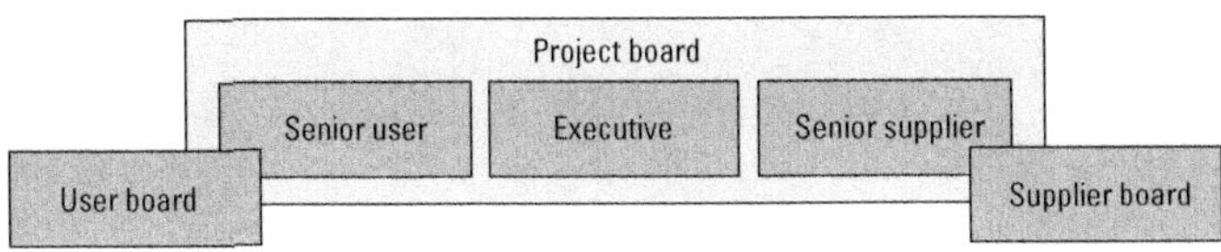

Figure 6.4 Project board with user and supplier boards

Project assurance – is the derivative responsibility of the project board. Project assurance monitors all aspects of the project's performance and products independently from the project manager, to release the individual board members from their supervision responsibilities. We distinguish separate business, user and supplier project assurance roles.

Members from the user and supplier boards can take up the project assurance role from the senior users and senior suppliers.

Change authority – is a delegated responsibility of the project board. The change authority is the person or group to which the project board delegates (partially) the responsibility for authorizing change requests and off-specifications.

Project manager – is responsible for the day-to-day management of the project on behalf of the project board. The project manager is responsible for the planning of the works, authorizing the work packages, monitoring the progress and taking corrective actions if necessary. If it is forecast that agreed tolerances will be exceeded, he has to escalate this to the project board for decision making. The project manager should align with project assurance. There is only one project manager.

Team manager – is responsible for ensuring the production of those products allocated to him by the project manager. The team manager reports to, and takes directions from, the project manager. The responsibility of the team manager to the project manager is a delegated responsibility from the senior supplier towards the executive. In many project there is more than one team manager.

Project support – is a derived responsibility of the project manager. Project support provides administrative services as well as specialist functions such as planning and budgetary control. Project support is typically responsible for configuration services and administrating change control.

PRINCE2 allows combining the project roles under the restriction that:

- The role of executive and project manager cannot be combined;
- There is only one executive and one project manager;
- The project assurance role cannot be delegated to the project manager, the project support or to one of the team managers.

6.6 Communication management approach

The communication management approach contains a description of the means and frequency of communication to internal and external stakeholders of the project. The approach is developed in the process initiating a project and is updated at the stage boundaries.

The project manager is responsible for documenting and maintaining the approach. The executive is accountable for the effectiveness of the approach. The actual communication activities are built into the appropriate plans and are monitored from there by the project manager.

6.7 Guidance for effective organization

Small project – Roles can, under restriction, be combined but not eliminated. Separate team managers, project assurance roles and project support roles may not be necessary. As the executive role and the senior user role are both from the customer environment, these roles can sometimes be combined.

Commercial projects – In commercial projects usually a separate supplier board is installed. The senior supplier is most often the account manager of the external supplier. When the external supplier is not yet contracted, the head of the purchase department can temporary fill in the senior supplier role.

Projects in a programme – In a programme a business change manager can fill in the role of senior user. The role of executive can be filled in by the programme manager. However this is only advisable for strategic projects.

Agile projects – In agile projects the team manager has a facilitating role (Scrum master). The voice of the user (senior user/change authority) is filled in by the product owner.

Chapter 7
Quality

7.1 Purpose of the quality theme

The purpose of the quality theme is to define and implement the means by which the project will verify that products are fit for purpose.

The quality theme defines the PRINCE2 approach to ensure that the project's products meet business expectations and that the desired benefits will subsequently be achieved.

The product focus is central to the PRINCE2 approach to quality, and is applicable to both management products and specialist products. Capturing and acting upon the lessons learnt contributes to the quality approach, as it is a means to continuous improvement.

7.2 Quality defined

Quality – is the degree to which a set of inherent characteristics of a product or process fulfils requirements, needs and expectations that are stated, self-evident or mandatory.

Customer quality expectations – the quality expected by the customer from the project product, captured in the project product description.

Acceptance criteria – criteria that the project product must meet before the customer will accept it.

Product description – is a description of a product's purpose, composition, derivation, quality criteria, how and by whom these criteria will be reviewed and who is responsible for approving the product.

Project product description – is a product description of the project product. This is used to gain agreement from the users about the scope, quality expectations and acceptance criteria for the project.

7.3 PRINCE2 requirements for the quality theme

A PRINCE2 project must, at a minimum:

- Define and maintain the quality management approach;
- Specify the customer quality expectations and prioritized acceptance criteria in the project product description;
- Specify quality criteria for products in their product descriptions;
- Initiate and maintain some form of quality register;
- Use lessons to inform quality.

7.4 Purpose of the quality management products

Quality management approach – The purpose of the quality management approach is to describe how quality will be managed on the project. This approach should cover minimally the project's approach to quality control and project assurance, how quality management is communicated throughout the project lifecycle and the roles and responsibilities for quality management.

Quality register – The purpose of the quality register is to summarize all the quality management activities that are planned or have taken place, the quality responsibilities, the quality results and the references to the respective quality records.

7.5 Quality management

Quality management is the whole of the coordinated activities required to direct and control an organization with regard to quality. A quality management system (QMS) is the complete set of quality standards, procedures and responsibilities for a site or organization.

In the project context, (host) sites and organizations are considered the (semi-) permanent organizations sponsoring the project work, either the corporate, programme management or customer.

The quality management approach in a project is derived from the QMSs of the respective customer and supplier organizations.

Quality planning – is the aspect of quality management that focuses on specifying the quality criteria and operational processes and resources to meet those quality criteria.

Quality control – is the aspect of quality management that focuses on ensuring compliance to the quality standards. Quality control includes all activities aimed at checking the project products to determine whether they comply with the relevant standards and identifying ways to eliminate causes of unsatisfactory performance.

Quality assurance – is the aspect of quality management that focuses on providing confidence that quality requirements will be met. Quality assurance consists of the setting up, monitoring and maintaining the quality management system in accordance to corporate, programme management or customer standards and policies.

Quality assurance is therefore independent of the project. Assurance of the quality inside the project conforming to PRINCE2 is part of the project assurance. Project and quality assurance are therefore conforming to PRINCE2, linked but independent responsibilities, see table 7.1.

Table 7.1 Relationship between project and quality assurance

Project assurance	Quality assurance
Assurance to the project's stakeholders that the project is being conducted appropriately and properly and complies with the plans and standards agreed	Assurance to corporate, programme management or customer that the project is conducted appropriately and properly and complies with the relevant corporate, programme management or customer standards and policies
Must be independent of the project manager and project team	Must be independent of the project management team
Responsibility of the project board	Responsibility of the corporate, programme management or customer
Quality assurance function can be used by the project board as part of the project assurance regime (e.g. to conduct quality audits)	Proper project assurance can provide confidence that the relevant corporate, programme management or customer standards and policies are met.

7.6 PRINCE2 approach to the quality theme

In quality planning we can distinguish the following steps:

- The customer quality expectations are first recorded in the project mandate;
- In the process starting up a project the customer quality expectations and the corresponding acceptance criteria are recorded in the project product description as part of the project brief;

- In the process initiating a project the project plan is drafted with the product descriptions of the main products. The project product description is updated, the quality management approach is defined and the quality register is initiated;
- In the process managing stage boundaries the stage plan is drafted with the product descriptions of the individual products. After approval of the stage plan the planned quality controls are recorded in the quality register.

With each further step in the project the criteria are specified in more detail. Criteria are specified in just enough detail to draft the respective plans. This approach enables projects to quick start and more freedom to adapt.

During managing product delivery, the team manager initiates the quality activities for the products to be delivered. These activities are based on the requirements that are documented in the product descriptions. This is part of quality control. The results of these quality control activities are recorded in the quality register. The quality records are filed in the quality dossiers.

Approval records – After sign off of the controlled products the products are approved, mostly by the senior user. This can be by a formal document or just by e-mail. These approval records must also be filed.

Acceptance records – At the closure of the project the project product is reviewed and accepted by the end-users as well as by operations and maintenance. These acceptance records will be filed as part of the documents to be handed over at the end of the project.

7.7 Guidance for effective quality management

Small project – Even in small projects you need to agree upfront about what criteria the products must meet. However the individual product descriptions can be replaced by an integrated programme of requirements.

Commercial projects – In commercial projects quality criteria are part of the contract between customer and supplier. Supplier tests must be distinguished from user tests.

Projects in a programme – A programme mainly focuses on process quality. A project mainly focuses on product quality. The project quality management approach is often determined by the programme management.

Agile projects – In agile projects features are described in user stories. Quality criteria for the individual features are described in a 'definition of done'. User tests are carried out at the end of each timebox. The results of these user tests can be documented in a kind of timebox review record.

7.8 Quality review technique

A quality review technique is a specific technique to assess whether a document or something similar is complete and adheres to the quality criteria agreed.

The objectives of a quality review are:

- Assess the conformity against the quality criteria;
- Provide confirmation that the product is complete and ready for approval;
- Provide a baseline for future change control;
- Promote wider acceptance of the product.

A quality review enforces stakeholder engagement, leadership, team building, development of individuals and a quality culture in the project.

A quality review distinguishes four roles:

- **Chair** – is responsible for the overall conduct of the review;
- **Presenter** – presents the producers of the product;
- **Reviewers** – review the product and confirm corrections;
- **Administrator** – records actions and results.

In preparation for the review the participants receive the respective document and the associated product description from the presenter. Attention points will be send to the chair for review. Small mistakes are annotated in the original and returned to the presenter.

Following the review the product can be signed off, (partly) disapproved or participants can agree to disagree. Often also change requests are initiated. Disputes and change requests are forwarded by the chair to the project manager for follow up.

7.9 Responsibilities quality theme

For the responsibilities of the quality theme, see table 7.2.

Table 7.2 Roles and responsibilities of the quality theme

Corporate, programme management or customer • Provide details of quality management system • Provide quality assurance **Executive** • Approve project product description • Approve quality management approach • Confirm acceptance of project product **Senior user** • Provide customer quality expectations and acceptance criteria and approve the PPD • Approve quality management approach • Approve PD's for key user products • Provide user resources for quality activities • Provide project product acceptance **Senior supplier** • Approve the PPD • Approve the quality management approach • Approve quality methods, techniques & tools • Approve PD's for key specialist products • Provide supplier resources for quality activities • PPD = Project product description • PD = Product description • PB = Project board	**Project manager (PM)** • Prepare PPD inclusive customer quality expectations and acceptance criteria • Prepare quality management approach • Prepare and maintain product descriptions • Ensure that TM's implement agreed quality control measures **Team manager (TM)** • Assist PM with preparing PD's • Produce products consistent with PD's • Manage quality controls for these products • Assemble quality records • Advise PM about product quality status **Project assurance** • Advise PM on quality management approach • Assist PB and PM on reviewing PD's • Advise PM on suitable quality reviewers • Assure PB on implementing quality management approach **Project support** • Provide administrative support for quality controls • Prepare and maintain quality register and quality records • Assist project team with application project quality processes

Chapter 8
Plans

8.1 Purpose of the plans theme

The purpose of the plans theme is to facilitate realization, communication and control by defining the means through which the products will be delivered.

8.2 Plans defined

A plan is a document, describing *how*, *when* and by *whom* a specific target or set of targets is to be achieved. Planning is the act or process of making and maintaining a plan.

PRINCE2 recommends three levels of plans to reflect the needs of the different levels of management involved in the project, see figure 8.1:

- Project plan;
- Stage plan;
- Team plan.

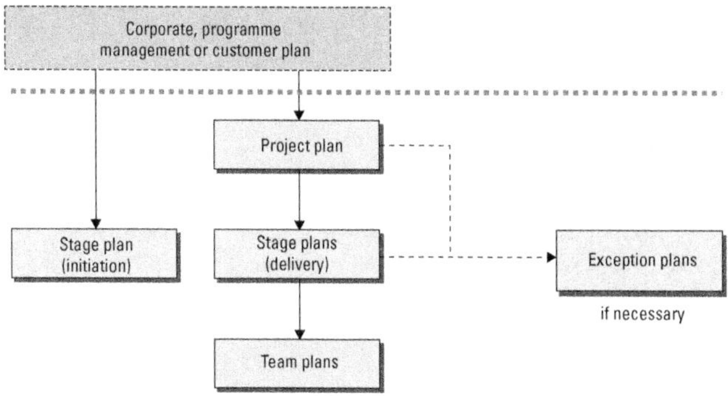

Figure 8.1 PRINCE2 planning levels (source: AXELOS Ltd.)

There is an initiation stage plan and there are one or more delivery stage plans. In addition PRINCE2 recognizes the exception plan, which is prepared in order to show the actions required to recover from the effect of a deviation.

Project plan – is used by the project board as a baseline against which to monitor a project's progress stage-by-stage. The project plan should align with the corporate, programme management or customer plan. The project plan identifies the milestones and management stages and provides the business case with planned project costs and timescales. The project plan is created in the initiation stage and is updated at the end of each management stage. The project plan is developed and maintained by the project manager and approved by the project board.

Stage plan – is required for each management stage. In its composition, the stage plan is similar to the project plan. The stage plan is the basis for the day-to-day control by the project manager. The next stage plan is produced near the end of the current management stage. For projects with only one delivery stage, the delivery stage plan can be incorporated in the project plan if the project plan covers the appropriate detail. The stage plan is developed and maintained by the project manager and is approved by the project board.

Team plan – is optional. If required it is created during the development of the parent stage plan, or when accepting a work package. The team plan is produced or amended by the team manager and is approved by the project manager. PRINCE2 does not describe the format or composition of a team plan. With external suppliers, a team plan often contains summary information intended to exercise control only. The senior supplier is accountable for the team plan.

Exception plan – will replace the plan in which deviations have occurred that are outside tolerance limits and will, after approval, become the new baselined project plan or stage plan. The format of the exception plan is the same as the plan it replaces. The exception plan covers the remaining period of the plan it replaces and will be approved by the next higher level of management.

8.3 PRINCE2 requirements for the plans theme

A PRINCE2 project must, at a minimum:

- Ensure that plans enable the business case to be realized;

- Have at least two management stages (initiation and one delivery stage);
- Produce a project plan for the project as a whole and a stage plan for each management stage; produce exception plans for managing exceptions;
- Use product-based planning for creating these plans;
- Define the roles and responsibilities for the planning;
- Use lessons to inform planning.

PRINCE2 requires that at least the following management products are produced and maintained:

- Project product description;
- Product descriptions;
- Product breakdown structure;
- Plans.

8.4 Management stages

Management stages are subdivisions in time, linked to go/no-go decisions with respect to the continuation of the project. Management stages are arranged sequentially.

There are at least two management stages in the project; the initiation stage and the delivery stage. The delivery stage can be split up into more than one management stage. The decision about the number of delivery management stages is taken during the initiation stage.

Delivery steps are characterized by the application of a set of techniques. Delivery steps can overlap. The number of delivery steps is normally larger than the number of management stages.

The number of management stages depends on:

- The planning horizon at any point in time;
- The key decisions points in the project;
- The alignment with corporate or programme activities;
- The amount of risk within the project;
- The benefits of too many short stages versus too few lengthy ones;
- How confident the board and the project manager are in proceeding.

If a management stage ends during a delivery step, it is necessary to split the delivery step up into a part before the go/no-go decision and a part after the go/no-go decision, see figure 8.2.

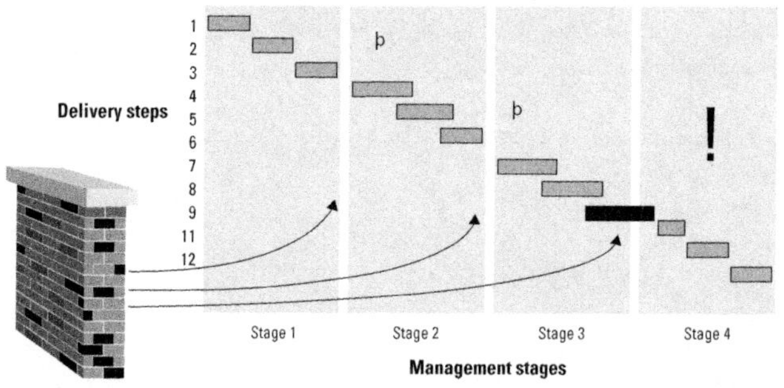

Figure 8.2 Management stages and delivery steps

8.5 PRINCE2 approach to the plans theme

The PRINCE2 approach to plans is that the required products are identified first, prior to the activities, dependencies and resources required. This is known as the product-based approach, see figure 8.3.

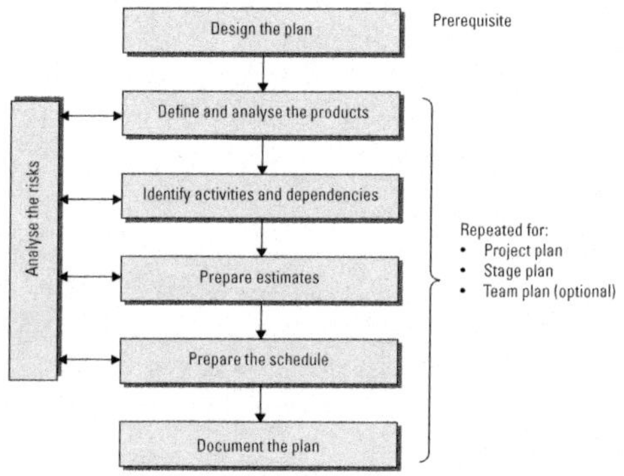

Figure 8.3 PRINCE2 approach to plans (source: AXELOS Ltd.)

Before plans can be developed, decisions have to be made about presentation and lay-out of the plans, the planning tools, estimating methods and levels. Any specific variations from the corporate, programme management or customer standards should be highlighted.

After the products have been identified and specified, the activities and dependencies between the activities can be identified, estimates can be made and a time schedule can be established. In parallel the identified risks should be analysed. Risk activities should be incorporated into the plan. Finally, the documents can be assembled and the plan documented.

8.6 Product-based planning approach

Defining and analyzing of the products can be done best with the product–based planning approach. The product-based planning approach comprises four steps, see figure 8.4.

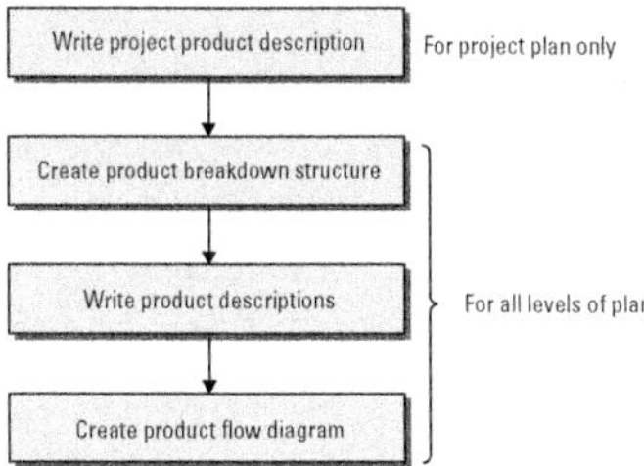

Figure 8.4 Product-based planning approach (source: AXELOS Ltd.)

Project product description – is the product description of the end product to be delivered by the project. The project product description describes the major product(s) to be delivered by the project, the source products from which the product is derived, the development skills needed, the customer quality expectations and acceptance criteria, the project tolerances and the acceptance methods and responsibilities.

The senior user is responsible for specifying the project product. In practice the project product description is written by the project manager in consultation with the executive and senior user.

Product breakdown structure (PBS) – is a hierarchy breakdown of all products to be produced in a plan. In a PBS we distinguish internal products, external products and product groups. External products are products that are needed in the project but already exists or are delivered by parties outside the project team. Product groups are not products on their own but just an indication of a specific group of products. External products and product groups should be distinguished in shape and or colour from the internal products. Also each external product should have a corresponding entry in the risk register.

It may be appropriate to identify intermediate states of a product as separate products, when the responsibility for creating the subsequent states will pass from one team to another.

Product description – is required for all identified products. A product description is written immediately after the product has been identified and will be frozen after the respective stage plan is approved. Although the project or team manager is responsible for writing the product descriptions, user representatives and material experts should be involved. A detailed requirement specification can be used as a substitute. External products may also require a product description

Product flow diagram (PFD) – defines the sequence in which the products will be developed and the interdependencies between them. The PFD can be created in parallel with PBS. All products, with the exception of external products and the start and end product, should have input and output relations. It is advisable to start the PFD from one single product or the PID. The end product is the project product. A PFD should not contain any loops. External products should be included, groupings not.

It is advisable to include also management products in the planning.

8.7 Guidance for effective planning

Small project – Small projects have mostly only one delivery stage. For small projects a project product description may be sufficient.

Commercial projects – The project plan should include procurement-related milestones. Both the customer and the supplier's plans may be confidential to the other party. Therefore it may be beneficial to prepare non-confidential versions of the plans that can be shared.

Projects in a programme – The number of management stages in a project can be influenced by the programme. The design of the plans can be prescribed by the programme.

Agile projects – A management stage can contain one or more releases/ increments. Work packages can contain one or more timeboxes. The product backlog corresponds with the project product description. The sprint backlogs correspond with the individual product descriptions.

8.8 Responsibilities plans theme

For the responsibilities of the plans theme, see table 8.1.

Table 8.1 Roles and responsibilities of the plans theme

<table>
<tr>
<td>
Corporate, programme management or customer
<ul>
<li>Provide corporate, programme management or customer planning standards</li>
<li>Define project tolerances in mandate</li>
<li>Approve project exception plans</li>
</ul>
Executive
<ul>
<li>Approve project plan</li>
<li>Define stage tolerances</li>
<li>Approve stage and exception plans</li>
<li>Commit business resources to stage plans</li>
</ul>
Senior user
<ul>
<li>Ensure project and stage plans remain consistent from user's perspective</li>
<li>Commit user resources to stage plans</li>
</ul>
Senior supplier
<ul>
<li>Ensure project and stage plans remain consistent from supplier perspective</li>
<li>Commit supplier resources to stage plans</li>
</ul>
</td>
<td>
Project manager (PM)
<ul>
<li>Design management stages and delivery steps</li>
<li>Develop project and stage plans</li>
<li>Prepare exception plan in response to exception deviations</li>
</ul>
Team manager (TM)
<ul>
<li>Create and update team plans</li>
<li>Prepare schedules for each work package</li>
</ul>
Project assurance
<ul>
<li>Review changes to the project plan on impact to the business case</li>
</ul>
Project support
<ul>
<li>Assist with development plans</li>
<li>Contribute with specialist expertise</li>
<li>Baseline, store and distribute plans</li>
</ul>
</td>
</tr>
</table>

Chapter 9
Risks

9.1 Purpose of the risk theme

The purpose of the risk theme is to identify, assess and control uncertainty and, as a result, improve the ability of the project to succeed.

Risk management should be systematic, focused on the proactive identification, assessment and control of risks. Effective risk management is a prerequisite to the continued business justification principle.

9.2 Risk defined

It is important to distinguish between risks and issues:

- **Issue** – a relevant event that has occurred and was not planned, and that requires management attention;
- **Risk** – an uncertain event or set of events that, if it occurs, will have an effect on the achievement of the objectives.

Risks can be divided into threats and opportunities:

- **Threat** – an uncertain event with a negative impact on objectives;
- **Opportunity** – an uncertain event with a positive impact on objectives.

A risk can have both a positive and a negative effect on objectives at the same time. Therefore threats and opportunities should be managed in conjunction.

Risk management is the systematic application of principles, approaches and processes to the tasks of identifying and assessing risk, planning and implementing risk responses and communicating risk management activities with stakeholders.

9.3 PRINCE2 requirements for the risk theme

A PRINCE2 project must, at a minimum:

- Create a risk management approach which at the very least covers:
  - How risks will be identified and managed throughout the project;

  - The roles and responsibilities for risk management;
  - How to assess whether risks will have a material impact on the business case;
- Create and maintain some form of risk register;
- Use lessons to inform risk identification and management.

9.4 PRINCE2 approach to the risk theme

The purpose of the key risk management products are:

- **Risk management approach** – describes how risks will be managed in the project. This includes the specific processes, procedures, techniques, standards and responsibilities to be applied;
- **Risk register** – provides a record of identified risks relating to the project, including their status and history.

A key decision that needs to be recorded in the approach is the project board's attitude towards risks (risk appetite), which in turn dictates the level of risk that is considered acceptable, and this is reflected in the risk tolerances.

Furthermore, the risk management approach describes levels of probability, impact and proximity, together with the risk response categories, early warning indicators and the risk budget.

The risk management approach is created by the project manager and approved by the executive. The risk register is created and maintained by the project support on behalf of the project manager.

9.5 Risk management procedures

The risk management procedure comprises the following five steps, see figure. 9.1.

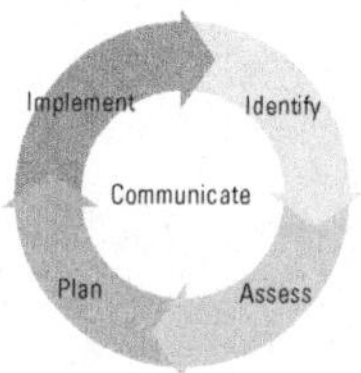

Figure 9.1 Risk management procedure (source: AXELOS Ltd.)

9.5.1 Identify:

- **Identify context** – obtain information about the project and identify the stakeholders in order to understand the specific objectives of the project plus formulate the risk management approach.

- **Identify risks** – capture the individual risks that may impact upon the project's objectives. Provide a clear and unambiguous expression of each risk by describing its cause, the risk itself (risk event) and the effect of the risk on the project's objectives, see figure 9.2.

Prepare early warning indicators to monitor critical aspects of the project. Provide information on the potential sources of risks. Assess the respective risk categories. Understand the stakeholders' view of the specific risks captured. Assign (temporary) risk owners. Record the risks in the risk register.

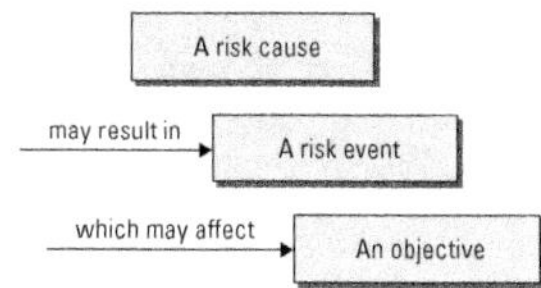

Figure 9.2 Risk cause, risk event and effect (based on: AXELOS Ltd.)

Project risks are risks which have an impact on the project's objectives and via that on the business. Business risks are risks which have a direct effect on the performance of the business itself.

9.5.2 Assess

Estimate – estimate the probability, impact and proximity, and the risk category of the individual risks. Confirm the assignment of the individual risk owners. Often the individual risks will be presented in a summary risk profile, see figure 9.3.

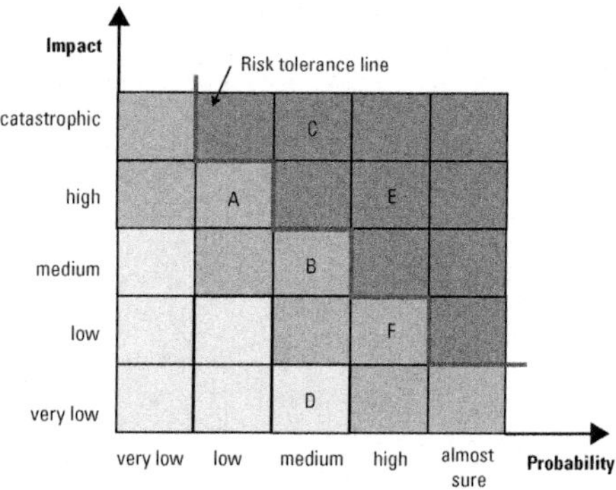

Figure 9.3 Example of summary risk profile

Evaluate – assess the net effect of all the individual risks on a project when aggregated together. This will enable the assessment whether the aggregated risks are within the defined risk tolerances and if the project has a continued business justification. Aggregated risks are often expressed in an expected monetary value, see table 9.1.

Table 9.1 Example of expected monetary value

Risk	Probability	Impact	Expected value
A	30%	€ 50.000,-	€ 15.000,-
B	60%	€ 25.000,-	€ 15.000,-
C	20%	€ 100.000,-	€ 20.000,-
Total	**Expected monetary value**		€ 50.000,-

The expected monetary value is often the basis for the risk budget. The risk budget is the budget to fund the risk responses should risks occur.

9.5.3 Plan

Identify and evaluate the different response options and their possible consequences for the project, see figure 9.4:

- **Avoid** – make sure the threat does not exist anymore;
- **Reduce** – reduce the probability or impact;
- **Contingency plan** – plan in advance what to do in case a risk materializes;
- **Transfer** – make a third party responsible (e.g. insurance);
- **Share** – choose a pain-gain formula;
- **Accept** – take the deliberate decision to monitor only;
- **Exploit** – materialize the opportunity;
- **Enhance** – increase probability or profit.

Risk	Threat responses	Opportunity responses
High ↑	Avoid	Exploit
	Reduce	Enhance
	Transfer	
	Share	
	Prepare contingency plan	
↓ Low	Accept	

Figure 9.4 Threats and opportunities responses (based on: AXELOS Ltd.)

An **inherent risk** is the risk before any action has been taken. A **residual risk** is the remaining risk after a risk action has been taken. A **secondary risk** is a risk caused by a risk response.

Build the individual responses into the appropriate plans after approval of the responses by the responsible authorities.

9.5.4 Implement

- Ensure that the role and responsibilities of the risk owners and risk actionees have been assigned, accepted and understood properly;
- Ensure that the planned risk responses are actioned;
- Monitor the effectiveness of the risk responses;
- Take corrective actions in case the responses are not effective.

Risk owner – an individual who is responsible for the management, monitoring and control of all aspects of a particular risk, including the risk responses. The risk owner reports on the risk to the project manager.

Risk actionee – an individual who is assigned to carry out a specific risk response in case the risk response is not in the remit of the risk owner. The risk actionee reports on the risk response to the risk owner.

9.5.5 Communicate

Communicate the status of the risks within the project management team and the external stakeholders. Risks should be an item of concern in every report and every meeting.

9.6 Guidance for effective risk management

Small project – In small projects the project manager will directly undertake most risk management activities, while in more complex projects these activities might be delegated to dedicated risk managers or to project support.

Commercial projects – In commercial projects there may be a need for more than one risk register and risk management approach. Where a joined risk register is used, care should be taken to appoint the correct risk owners.

Projects in a programme – The project risk management approach can be derived from the risk management approach of the programme. The risk register of the project should be linked to the risk register of the programme.

Agile projects – In agile projects the risk of delivering unwanted products is minimalized, but there is still the risk that the results do not align with corporate strategy. Be aware: failure to properly organize agility in projects, can pose risks in itself.

9.7 Responsibilities risk theme

For the responsibilities of the risk theme, see table 9.2.

Table 9.2 Roles and responsibilities of the risk theme

Corporate, programme management or customer / Executive / Project board / Senior user / Senior supplier	Project manager (PM) / Team manager (TM) / Project assurance / Project support / Risk owner / Risk actionee
Corporate, programme management or customer • Provide risk management policy • Provide risk management process guide	**Project manager (PM)** • Create the risk management approach • Create and maintain risk register • Responsible for management of risks
Executive • Approve risk management approach • Responsible for business risks • Escalate risk to corporate, programme management or customer	**Team manager (TM)** • Participate in identifying, assessing and controlling risks **Project assurance** • Review risk management practices • Ensure alignment with approach
Project board • Inform PM about external risks • Take decision on risks	**Project support** • Assist PM in maintaining risk register
Senior user • Ensure risk related to user aspects are managed	**Risk owner** • Management of individual risk
Senior supplier • Ensure risks related to supplier aspects are managed	**Risk actionee** • Carry out risk response action

Chapter 10
Change

10.1 Purpose of the change theme

The purpose of the change theme is to identify, assess and control any potential and approved issues and changes to the project baselines.

The purpose of change control is not to prevent changes. It is to ensure that every change is approved by the relevant authority before it takes place. Changes have a direct impact on the product descriptions.

10.2 Change defined

Change control – the procedure which ensures that all issues and changes that may affect the project's objectives are identified, assessed, and either approved, rejected or deferred.

Issue – a relevant but unplanned event that has happened or most probably will happen, and requires management action.

Change – the alteration of a baseline. A baseline is a reference level against which an entity is monitored and controlled. By definition, therefore, a change is a specific issue.

PRINCE2 recognizes three types of issues:
- **Request for change** – a proposal for change of a baseline;
- **Off-specification** – a product that doesn't comply or is not expected to comply;
- **Problem/concern** – any other issue that the project manager needs to resolve or escalate.

Configuration management (CM) – the technical and administrative activity concerned with the creation, maintenance and controlled change of a configuration item.

Configuration item (CI) – an entity that is subject to configuration management. The entity may be a component of a product, a product, or a set of products in a release.

10.3 PRINCE2 requirements for the change theme

A PRINCE2 project must, at a minimum:

- Define a change control approach which at the very least covers:
  - How issues will be identified and managed throughout the project;
  - The roles and responsibilities for change control;
  - How it will be assessed whether changes will have a material impact on the business case;
- Create and maintain some form of issue register;
- Use lessons to inform issue identification and management.

10.4 PRINCE2 approach to the change theme

The project's controls for issues and changes are defined and established in the initiation stage, see chapter 13, and reviewed and updated towards the end of each intermediate management stage.

Management products used to establish and maintain change control and issue management are:

Change control approach – describes how to identify, assess and control any issue and potential and approved change to a product baseline. It describes the procedures, techniques and standards to be applied, the scales for priority and severity and the responsibilities for issue management and change control.

A widely recognized scale for priority and severity is the **MoSCoW**-technique: Must have – Should have – Could have – Won't have for now.

Issue register – to capture and maintain information on all issues that are formally managed. The issue register should be monitored by the project manager on a regular basis.

Issue report – for each issue captured in the issue register, an issue report should be created. An issue report contains all the relevant information including the impact analysis in relation to the respective issue.

Configuration-item-record – a record that describes the status and version of a configuration item and the dependencies with other configuration items. Configuration items records are usually stored in a configuration management database (CMDB).

Product status account – a report on the status of products. This report is particularly useful if the project manager wishes to confirm the version and status of the configuration items, e.g. at the end of a management stage, at the end of the project, or as part of examining issues and risks.

Daily log – the project diary for the project manager. In this context it is used to record problems/concerns that can be handled informally.

10.5 Issue and change control procedure

The issue and change control procedure comprises five steps, see figure 10.1.

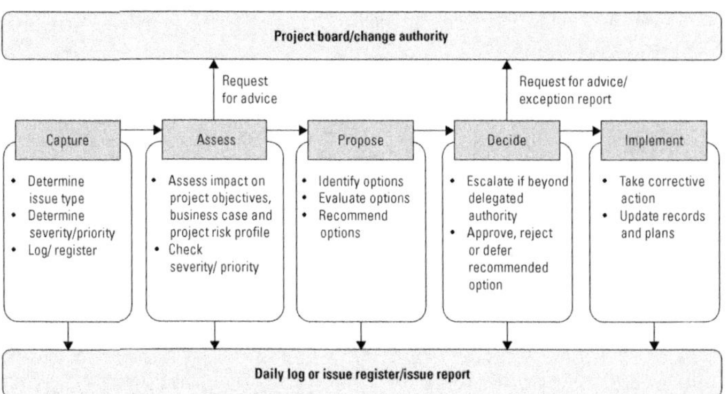

Figure 10.1 Issue and change control procedure (source: AXELOS Ltd.)

1. **Capture** – determine if an issue can be handled informally or not. Determine the type, severity and priority of the issue. Log the issues which should be handled formally in the issue register. Draft an issue report to capture the information already known about the issue.

2. **Assess** – assess the impact on project objectives, project risk profile and the busines case from business, user and supplier perspectives. Check the severity and priority and if required, request advice.

3. **Propose** – identify and evaluate options, including the cost-benefit of each option in relation to the interests of the project and its stakeholders.

4. **Decide** – decide upon the corrective actions to be taken. Forward requests for change to the respective change authority. Escalate an exception report if issues are forecast to exceed agreed tolerances.

The project board can:

- Approve the change or accept the off-specification without corrective actions (concession);
- Reject the change or instruct the off-specification to be resolved;
- Defer the decision to a later date;
- Request more information;
- Provide guidance for a problem or concern;
- Ask for an exception plan.

5. **Implement** – carry out the necessary corrective actions. Draft an exception plan if so directed by the project board.

At each step, update the issue register and issue report and inform the person who raised the issue accordingly.

Change authority – It is the project boards responsibility to review and approve requests for change and off-specifications. However this can be quite time consuming and often requires specialist knowledge. It may therefore be appropriate to delegate some decisions to a person or group, called the change authority.

The project manager can be made responsible for minor changes. Sometimes a change advisory board (CAB) is installed.

Change budget – The change authority can be allocated a change budget to finance authorized requests for change. This prevents costs of changes being charged to the contingency or delivery budget.

In all instances, when possible changes are forecast to exceed the agreed tolerances, changes should be referred back to the project board for decision.

10.6 Guidance for effective change control

Small project – In small projects the project manager will directly undertake most issue and change control activities, in more complex projects these activities might be delegated to project support.

Commercial projects – The project may require to adopt the change control procedures and processes defined in the contract. Issue management and change control may be treated as separate processes and procedures depending on the regulations set in the contract.

Projects in a programme – The project may require to adopt the issue and change control procedures defined in the programme. Also, the change authority and the change budget may be set by the programme.

Agile projects – The change authority is the product owner. All changes are prioritized. As timeboxes end, the lower prioritized features which are not yet realized, will fall due automatically (exchange principle). Therefore in agile projects no change budget is necessary.

10.7 Responsibilities change theme

For the responsibilities of the change theme, see table 10.1.

Table 10.1 Responsibilities of the change theme

Corporate, programme management or customer Provide corporate, programme management or customer strategy for issue management and change control **Executive** • Approve change control approach: • Set scales for severity & priority • Determine change authority/budget • Respond to request for advice • Take decisions on issues **Senior user/ supplier** • Respond to request for advice • Take decisions on issues **Project assurance** • Advice on change control approach • Advice on examining and resolving issues	**Project manager (PM)** • Create and maintain change control approach • Manage issue and change control procedures, assisted by project support • Create and maintain issue register, assisted by project support • Implement corrective actions **Team manager (TM)** • Implement issue and change control procedures within his work package • Implement corrective actions **Project support** • Assist the PM with issue and change control procedures • Assist the PM to maintain issue register • Maintain configuration item records, if used • Produce product status accounts

Chapter 11
Progress

11.1 Purpose of the progress theme

The purpose of the progress theme is to establish a mechanism by which to monitor and compare actual achievements against those planned, provide a forecast for the project's objectives and its continued viability, and control any unacceptable deviations.

The progress theme provides a mechanism for the continued business justification, managing on a stage-by-stage basis and by exception.

11.2 Progress defined

Progress – the measure of the achievements of the objectives of a plan.
Tolerance – the permissible deviation from a plan's objectives without the need to escalate the deviation to the next management level.
Exception – a situation where it is forecast that there will be a deviation beyond the agreed tolerance levels.

Progress controls ensure that for each level of the project management team, the next level of management can:

- Monitor progress;
- Compare achievements against plans;
- Review plans and options against future situations;
- Detect problems and identify risks;
- Initiate corrective actions;
- Authorize further work.

11.3 PRINCE2 requirements for the progress theme

A PRINCE2 project must, at a minimum:

- Define its approach to control progress;
- Manage stage by stage;
- Set tolerances and manage by exception;

- Review business justification when exceptions are raised;
- Use lessons to improve progress control.

11.4 Management by exception

- The project board meets at decision points only, with intermediate advice and direction when needed;
- The project board delegates the assurance that the project is being conducted properly to the project assurance;
- The project board delegates responsibility for the consideration of requests for change to a change authority;
- The project board delegates the day-to-day management to the project manager within set tolerances, with highlight reports produced at agreed intervals;
- The project manager issues an exception report when it is forecast that agreed tolerance levels are likely to be exceeded.

11.5 PRINCE2 approach to the progress theme

PRINCE2 provides progress control through:

- Dividing the project in management stages (see chapter 9, Plans);
- Delegating authority;
- Event- and time-driven reports and reviews;
- Raising exceptions.

11.6 Delegating authority

PRINCE2 recognizes six basic performance areas to be managed. Tolerances have to be defined for each performance area for the respective level of management, see figure 11.1.

Control aspects	Project level tolerances	Stage level tolerances	Work package level tolerances
Time	Project plan	Stage plan	Work package
Cost	Project plan	Stage plan	Work package
Scope	Project plan	Stage plan	Work package
Risk	Risk managment approach	Stage plan	Work package
Quality	Project product description	Product description	Product description
Benefits	Business case	NA	NA

Figure 11.1 The six tolerance types per management level (based on: AXELOS Ltd.)

11.7 Event- and time-driven controls

PRINCE2 recognizes:

- **Event-driven controls** – at the end of a stage (end stage report), at the end of the project (end project report) and when an exception is raised (exception report);
- **Time-driven controls** – at predefined periodic intervals, such as checkpoint reports and highlight reports.

Baselines for progress controls are:

- **Project plan** – is used by the project board to monitor a project's progress on a stage-by-stage basis;
- **Stage plan** – is the basis for the day-to-day control by the project manager;
- **Exception plan** – shows actions required to recover from the effect of a tolerance deviation;
- **Work packages** – authorized by the project manager to a team manager to undertake project works during a stage.

Reviewing progress:

- **Daily log** – the personal diary of the project manager. This is useful for recording actions and problems/concerns that can be handled informally;
- **Issue register and issue report** – to capture and manage formal requests for change off-specifications and other issues/problems;
- **Product status account** – to provide a status of the products. This is especially of interest if the project manager wants to verify the status and the versions of the products;
- **Quality register** – to record all planned and implemented quality activities and to act as a pointer to quality records;
- **Risk register** – to record all identified risks, and risk responses.

Informal records are captured in logs. Formal records are captured in registers.

Capturing and reporting lessons:

- **Lessons log** – to capture previous lessons from earlier projects and also the lessons learned during the course of the project itself;
- **Lessons report** – to forward lessons which will be of interest to other projects. Lessons reports can be forwarded at stage ends and at project closure.

Reporting on progress:

- **Checkpoint reports** – produced by the team manager at agreed intervals to enable the project manager to review work package status;
- **Highlight reports** – produced by the project manager at agreed intervals to enable the project board to manage stages by exception. The highlight report can also be sent to other stakeholders as documented in the communication management approach;
- **End stage reports** – produced by the project manager at the end of a stage to enable the project board to evaluate the previous stage and to authorize the project's continuation;
- **End project report** – produced by the project manager at the end of the project to enable the project board to evaluate the project and authorize project closure.

The project's controls are documented in the project initiation documentation (PID), the stage controls in the stage plan and the controls for the team manager in the work packages.

11.8 Raising exceptions

When it is forecast that agreed tolerances will be exceeded, an exception should be raised to the next management level, see figure 11.2:

- **Work package-level exceptions** – the team manager raises an issue to the project manager;
- **Stage-level exceptions** – the project manager escalates an exception report to the project board;
- **Project-level exceptions** – the project board forwards the exception report to corporate, programme management or customer for a decision.

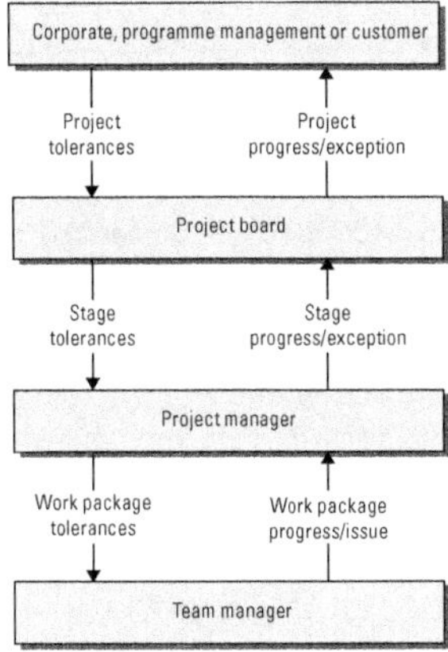

Figure 11.2 The four levels of control (source: AXELOS Ltd.)

Based on the exception report the project board instructs the project manager to postpone the exception, close the project prematurely or produce an exception plan or increases the tolerance.

11.9 Guidance for effective progress control

Small project – In small projects the progress of individual work packages is generally reported verbally in a joined team meeting and is directly registered in the current stage plan. In more complex projects earned value analyses are mostly used to analyse and report progress.

Commercial projects – In commercial projects progress reports are mostly defined in the contract. Attention should be paid to how the external supplier should report progress, so the client can exercise proper project control.

Projects in a programme – If a project is part of a programme, the programme usually set the project tolerances and mandates the progress controls for the project.

Agile projects – In agile projects usually Kanban boards and burn down charts are used to visualize the progress. Benefits tolerances are set by defining the minimal marketable product (MMP) to be delivered, given a fixed cost, time and quality.

11.10 Responsibilities progress theme

For responsibilities of the progress theme, see table 11.1.

Table 11.1 Roles and responsibilities of the progress theme

Corporate, programme management or customer • Provide project tolerances in mandate • Decide upon project exception reports **Executive** • Provide stage tolerances • Decide upon stage exception reports • Ensure that progress towards the outcome remains consistent from business perspective • Recommend future actions to corporate, programme management or customer based on project exception reports **Senior user** • Ensure that progress towards the outcome remains consistent from user perspective **Senior supplier** • Ensure that progress towards the outcome remains consistent from supplier perspective	**Project manager (PM)** • Authorize work packages • Monitor progress against stage plan • Produce highlight and end stage reports • Produce exception reports • Maintain project's registers and logs **Team Manager (TM)** • Agree work package with PM • Inform project support about quality checks • Produce checkpoint reports • Notify PM about forecast deviation from tolerances **Project assurance** • Monitor changes to the project plan in terms of impact on the business case • Confirm stage and project progress against agreed tolerances **Project support** • Assist with compilation of reports • Contribute with specialist expertise • Maintain issue, risk and quality register on behalf of the PM

PART III PROCESSES

Chapter 12
Introduction to PRINCE2 processes

PRINCE2 is a process-based approach to project management. There are seven processes in PRINCE2, which provide the set of activities required to direct, manage and deliver a project successfully. A process delivers output(s) to which one or more inputs are needed.

The seven processes are, see figure 12.1:

- Starting up a project (SU);
- Directing a project (DP);
- Initiating a project (IP);
- Controlling a stage (CS);
- Managing product delivery (MP);
- Managing a stage boundary (SB);
- Closing a project (CP).

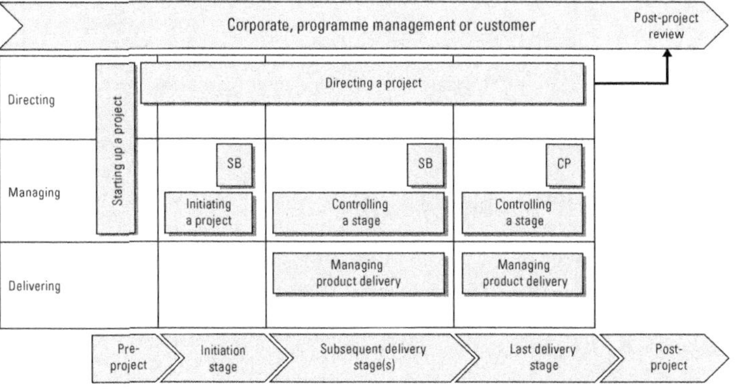

Figure 12.1 Process overview (based on: AXELOS Ltd.)

Each process contains a structured set of activities that accomplishes specific objectives. The PRINCE2 processes will be explained in the following chapters. Each chapter describes the purpose, the objectives, the context and the activities of the respective process.

Each process is viewed from the project manager's perspective, except the processes directing a project (project board's perspective) and managing product delivery (team manager's perspective).

A project can include several management stages: one initiation stage and multiple delivery stages. For a simple project there may be only two management stages: an initiation stage and one delivery stage. The pre-project and the post-project stages – as the terms indicate – are not part of the project.

12.1 Pre-project

The trigger to start a project is provided by the corporate, programme management or customer and can be caused by a change in legislation, new business objectives or any other threat or opportunity. This trigger, the project mandate, can vary from a verbal instruction to an extensive project description.

However prior to initiating the project, it is essential to ensure first that the prerequisites for initiation are in place. This is taken care of in the process starting up a project. The output of this process is a project brief and an initiation stage plan. Based on these documents the project board can then authorize (in the directing a project process) the initiation of the project.

12.2 Initiation stage

In the initiating a project process the project management approaches are defined, the project delivery is planned and the business case is refined to establish a solid foundation for the project, enabling the organization to understand the work that needs to be done and to assure that the project is viable, desirable and achievable.

The initiation stage cumulates in the project initiation documentation (PID) which is reviewed by the project board (in the directing a project process) to decide whether to authorize the project. The managing a stage boundary process is used to plan the next management stage in detail.

12.3 Subsequent delivery stage(s)

The project board delegates the day-to-day control to the project manager on a stage-by-stage basis. The project manager ensures that progress is in line with the stage plan and stays within its tolerances and that the work is carried out according to the specification (controlling a stage process). The team accepts and executes the assigned work packages (managing product delivery process).

Towards the end of each stage the project manager reports about the stage performance, updates the project plan and business case, prepares the next stage plan and requests permission from the project board to proceed with the next stage (managing a stage boundary process).

12.4 Final delivery stage

After execution and approval of the final products in the controlling a stage process, the supplier can hand over the project product to the customer and the project manager can decommission the project in the closing a project process. The project resources can be released. The project files should be tidied up and archived. The project administration should be closed. The business case and the benefits management approach should be updated. The project performance should be assessed and the lessons learned and any follow-on recommendations should be documented and handed over to the parties concerned (closing a project process).

12.5 Post-project

After putting the project product into operational use the perceived outcome can be achieved and the expected benefits can be realized and measured by the corporate, programme management or customer, based on the updated benefits management approach. If the project is part of a programme, the benefit reviews will be part of the programme's benefits management activities.

12.6 Tailoring the processes

PRINCE2 requires that the project management processes reflect the needs of the project but are as simple as possible. Project management activities can be omitted, the processe itself cannot.

Chapter 13
Starting up a project

13.1 Purpose

The purpose of this process is to ensure that the prerequisites for initiating a project are in place by answering the question whether or not the project is considered viable and worthwhile. This process is lighter than the more thorough initiating a project process. The aim is to do the minimum necessary to decide whether it is worthwhile to even start the initiation of the project.

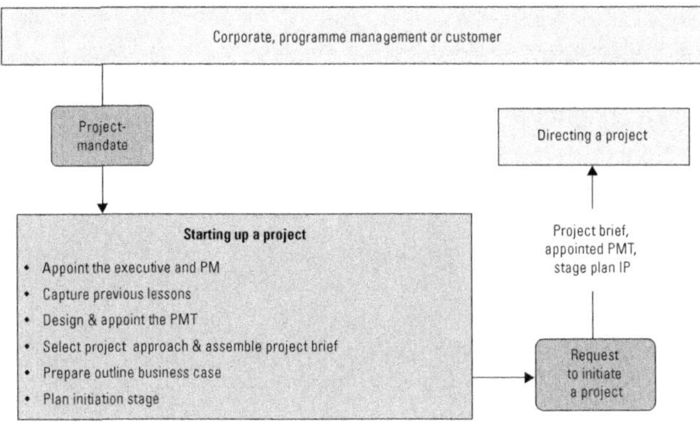

Figure 13.1 Starting up a project process

13.2 Objective

The objective of starting up a project process is to ensure that:

- There is a business justification, and all the necessary authorizations exist for initiating the project;
- There is sufficient information to define and confirm the scope and select the approach of the project;
- People are appointed who will execute the initiation stage or have a significant project management role in the project;

- The work for the initiation is planned;
- Time is not wasted initiating a project based on unsound assumptions.

13.3 Context

The trigger for the project is the project mandate, which is provided by the corporate, programme management or customer. They also appoint the executive which in turn appoints the project manager. Based on the project mandate and in agreement with the executive, the project manager develops the project brief including the previous lessons, the project management team, the project approach and an outline business case. In addition he drafts the plan for the initiation stage, see figure 13.1.

Based on the project brief and the initiation stage plan the project board may authorize the initiation of the project in the directing a project process.

13.4 Activities

13.4.1 Appoint the executive and the project manager

To get anything done in the project, a decision maker with the appropriate authority and someone who will manage the project on a day-to-day basis are needed. The following actions are recommended:

- Review the project mandate and check the understanding;
- Appoint the executive (by the corporate, programme management or customer);
- Appoint the project manager (by the executive);
- Create the daily log, as a repository for project information.

13.4.2 Capture previous lessons

Previous projects or programmes can provide useful lessons about processes, techniques and estimates for the project. The following actions are recommended:

- Create the lessons log;
- Review related lessons reports from similar previous projects that can be applied to this project. These lessons may also come from corporate, programme management or customer and external organizations;
- Consult people with previous experience of similar projects;
- Record any lessons identified in the lessons log.

13.4.3 Design and appoint the project management team

The project requires the right people to make decisions in a timely manner. And the project needs a project management team that reflects the interests of parties involved. The following actions are recommended:

- Review the lessons log for lessons related to the project management team structure;
- Design the project management team, including role descriptions and project management team structure, and consider any role combinations;
- Appoint the project management team;
- Estimate the time and effort required for each role and identify potential candidates;
- Confirm the individual candidate's availability and role comprehension and assign the selected people;
- If any risks are identified, add them to the daily log.

13.4.4 Prepare the outline business case

A crucial element in the project is WHY the project is needed. A high-level view of the business case is appropriate at this time. If the project is part of a programme, the business case may already have been identified at programme level. The following actions are recommended:

- Draft the outline business case based on what's currently known about the project;
- Consult the executive and senior user to define what the project is to deliver, and create the project product description;
- Review the risks captured in the daily log and summarize the key risks affecting the project's viability in the outline business case.

13.4.5 Select the project approach and assemble the project brief

Before any planning activities are undertaken, decisions will be made about how the work is going to be approached. An agreed project brief ensures a commonly understood and well-defined starting point. The following actions are recommended:

- Evaluate possible delivery solutions and decide upon the approach appropriate to delivering the project product and achieving the outline business case;
- Define requirements on tailoring, if known at this time;
- Assemble the project brief by confirming and incorporating the products from previous activities in this process and by identifying constraints, assumptions, project tolerances, user(s) and any other parties, and the interfaces the project must maintain.

13.4.6 Plan the initiation stage

The effort and deliverables for the initiation stage need to be planned. If not, the initiation can be aimless and unstructured. The following actions are recommended:

- Decide upon suitable management controls for the initiation stage;
- Identify any constraints on time and costs for the initiation stage and produce the initiation stage plan;
- Review risks and issues in the daily log and assess their impact on the initiation stage plan
- Identify any new risks and issues and update if the daily log is needed;
- Request authorization to initiate the project.

13.5 Tailoring starting up a project

Simple project – In a simple project this process can be done in a more informal way, but should not be bypassed. The project brief can be just an elaboration of the project mandate and recorded in the minutes of the meeting between the project manager and the executive.

Agile project – In an agile project the purpose of the project is defined and the hypotheses on which the delivery of the project will be based, will be tested. Further it will be decided in which agile way of working the project will be carried out.

Commercial project – When the project is run from a supplier's perspective the starting up a project process (pre-contract) is usually done in response to a customer's request for proposal.

Project within a programme – If the project is part of the programme, the programme manager appoints the executive and project manager, and generally will already provide a draft project brief. Still the project manager has to make sure that the project brief is complete and comprehensive and that the project is viable and worthwhile initiating.

Chapter 14
Directing a project

14.1 Purpose

The purpose of this process is to enable the project board to be accountable for the project's success by making key decisions and exercising overall control, while delegating the day-to-day management to the project manager.

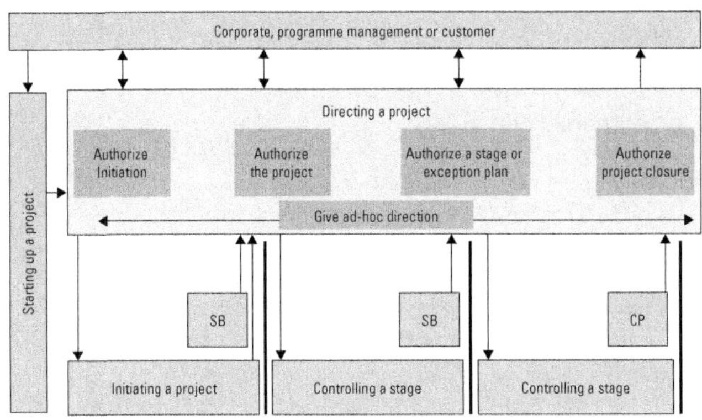

Figure 14.1 Directing a project process

14.2 Objective

The objective of the directing a project process is to ensure that:

- There is authority to initiate the project, to deliver the project product and to close the project;
- Management direction and control are provided throughout the project and that there is assurance that the project remains viable;
- Corporate, programme management or customer has an interface to the project;
- Plans for realizing post-project benefits are managed and reviewed.

14.3 Context

This process views the project from the project board's perspective and is triggered by th project manager's request to initiate the project, as shown in figure 14.1. The project boar manages by exception and monitors through reports and through controls at decision point There is no necessity for intermediate progress meetings.

The project board communicates with corporate, programme management or customer an assures that there is continued business justification. The project board and project manage should not only provide formal but also informal communication when needed.

14.4 Activities

14.4.1 Authorize initiation

With this activity the project board ensures that the investment that is to be made i worthwhile. The following actions are recommended:

- Review and approve the project brief including the project product description and th initiation stage plan;
- Verify that the outline business case demonstrates a viable project;
- Inform stakeholders and the host site(s) that the project is being initiated and reques any required support;
- Authorize the project manager to proceed with the initiation stage.

14.4.2 Authorize the project

This activity will be triggered by a request from the project manager for the authorization to deliver the project and should be performed in parallel with the authorization of a stage or exception plan. Should the project board not authorize the project at this point, the project will be closed prematurely. The following actions are recommended:

- Review and approve the PID and benefits management approach;
- Notify corporate, programme management or customer, the host site(s) and other interested parties that the project has been authorized;
- Authorize the project manager to deliver the project or to close the project prematurely.

14.4.3 Authorize a stage or exception plan

When a management stage nears its end or an exception plan has been drafted, the project board reviews the performance of the current stage, reviews the updated project plan and business case and authorizes the next stage or the exception plan if they are convinced of the continued viability of the project. The following actions are recommended:

- Review and approve the end stage report;
- Review and approve the stage plan or exception plan;
- Authorize the project manager to proceed with the submitted plans, or ask the project manager to revise the plans when rejected, or instruct the project manager to close the project prematurely;
- Communicate the status of the project to corporate, programme management or customer.

14.4.4 Give ad hoc direction

Project board members may give guidance or respond to requests for advice at any time during the project. Triggers for such actions can be:

- Informal requests for advice and guidance;
- An escalated issue or exception report;
- The receipt of a highlight report;
- Advice from corporate, programme management or customer.

Responses from project board (members) can be:

- Assist the project manager as required;
- Make a decision within the limits of authority;
- Defer the decision or request more information;
- Seek advice from corporate, programme management or customer;
- Instruct the project manager to produce an exception plan or to close the project prematurely.

14.4.5 Authorize project closure

Every project needs a controlled closure where the project board has to assess whether the objectives have been achieved or that the project has nothing more to contribute and has to review the project performance. The following actions are recommended:

- Verify the handover of the project product and the acceptance by the user, operation and maintenance, in conformity with the project product description;
- Confirm the updated business case and benefits management approach and the transfe to corporate, programme management or customer;
- Confirm the lessons report and the follow-on actions recommendations and the transfe to corporate, programme management or customer;
- Review and approve the end project report including a summary of the deviations from the approved plans;
- Review and issue a project closure notification.

14.5 Tailoring directing a project

Simple project – The directing of a simple project may be less formal. If the project has only one delivery stage the activity of authorizing a stage plan is not needed.

Agile project – The project board may attend demos, ensuring that decision-making is based on information gathering rather than formal reporting. Since time and costs are fixed when using agile, this information focuses primarily on the scope and the quality of the delivered functionality.

Commercial project – The external supplier may provide a person as senior supplier in the project board or may participate in a supplier board chaired by the senior supplier.

Project within a programme – The senior user may be one of the business change managers at the programme. In incidental cases the executive may be the programme manager.

Chapter 15
Initiating a project

15.1 Purpose

The purpose of this process is to establish solid foundations for the project, enabling the organization to understand the work that needs to be done to deliver the project product, before committing to a significant expenditure.

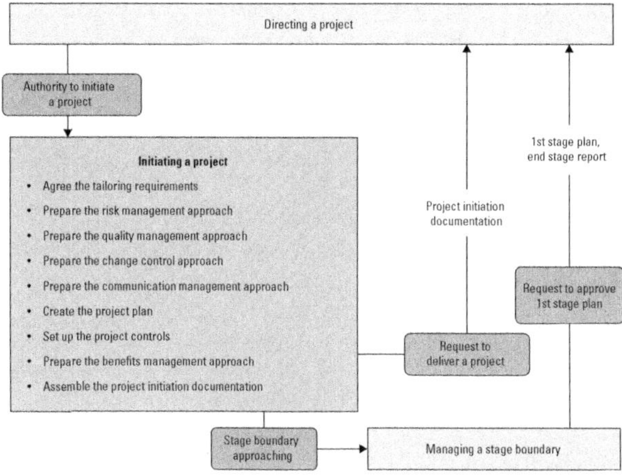

Figure 15.1 Initiating a project process

15.2 Objective

The objective of the initiating a project process is to ensure there is a common understanding of:

- Why the project is needed, the benefits expected and the associated risks;
- The scope of the works and the products to be delivered;
- How, when and what is to be delivered, and at what cost;

- Who is involved in the project decision making;
- How the required quality will be achieved;
- How baselines will be established and controlled;
- How risks, issues and changes will be identified, assessed and controlled;
- How progress will be monitored and controlled;
- Who needs which information and in which format and at what time;
- How the corporate, programme management or customer standards will be tailored to suit the project.

15.3 Context

This process starts with the authorization of the initiation by the project board in the directing a project process, based on the project brief and the initiation stage plan. This process describes how the project manager lays down the foundations for a successful project, by drafting the project plan, refining the business case and creating the suite of management products required for control purposes, all combined forming the project initiation documentation, see figure 15.1.

The initiating the project process triggers the managing a stage boundary process for creating the stage plan for the first delivery stage and the end stage report of the initiation stage.

The initiating a project process enables the project board to direct the project process authorizing the (delivery of) the project, in coordination with the corporate, programme management or customer.

15.4 Activities

15.4.1 Agree the tailoring requirements

The project manager needs to tailor how the project will be directed and managed because of internal and external factors. When deviating from the organization's project management approach it should be agreed and documented. The following actions are recommended:

- If defined in the project brief, review the outline tailoring approach;
- Seek lessons related to how tailoring needs to be applied;
- Define the tailoring and create the initial project controls;

- Consult with project assurance to assure that tailoring meets the needs of the project board and corporate, programme management or customer;
- Seek approval from the project board.

15.4.2 Prepare the management approaches

Prepare the risk, quality and communication management approach and the change control approach. Management approaches describe the procedures, tools, records and reporting, timing and responsibilities for the respective aspects of the project.

The following actions are recommended:

- Review the tailoring approach and the implications this has for the management approaches;
- Review the project brief, look for lessons and check whether any corporate, programme management or customer strategies, standards or practices related to these approaches need to be applied;
- Review the project product description to understand the customer quality expectations;
- Define the management approaches;
- Consult with project assurance whether the approaches meet the needs of project board and corporate, programme management or customer;
- Create the risk and issue register and update these with the identified risks and issues;
- Create the quality register for recording upcoming quality activities;
- Create the initial configuration item records for recording upcoming configuration items, if used;
- Seek approval from the project board.

15.4.3 Create the project plan

The timescales, resource requirements and cost estimates are needed for the project board's control and the refinement of the business case. The project manager should undertake this activity with close involvement of the user(s) and supplier(s). The following actions are recommended:

- Review the project brief and look for lessons;
- Review the tailoring approach and its implications for the planning;
- Review the risk and issue register for risks and issues concerning planning;
- Decide on the format and presentation of the project plan;

- Identify any planning and control tools to be used;
- Choose the method of estimating;
- Create a product breakdown structure, product flow diagram and product description for the major products;
- Check if the project product description needs to be updated;
- Create or update the configuration item records, if used;
- Identify and confirm resources required, and check their availability, role acceptance and role commitment;
- Set up the time schedule and define the time and cost budgets, including provisions for risks and changes;
- Document the project plan;
- Consult with project assurance whether the project plan meets the needs of the project board and corporate, programme management or customer;
- Update the relevant logs and registers if necessary;
- Seek approval from the project board.

15.4.4 Set up the project controls

The required levels of control between project board, project manager and team manager need to be established before the project commences its execution. The following actions are recommended:

- Review the tailoring approach and the implications this has for controls;
- Look for lessons learned and review logs and registers for related issues and risks as they can affect the rigour of control activities;
- Review the approaches to identify which controls need to be established;
- Confirm the management stage boundaries;
- Allocate the different levels of decision-making;
- Confirm the tolerances and the escalation procedures;
- Consult with project assurance whether the controls meet the needs of the project board and corporate, programme management or customer;
- Update the relevant logs and registers if necessary;
- Seek approval from the project board.

15.4.5 Prepare the benefits management approach

The outline business case needs to be updated with the project plan's estimates on time, cost and risks. The detailed business case is needed for the project board's decision as to whether the project is and remains viable. The following actions are recommended:

- Review the project brief and look for lessons;
- Review the tailoring approach and its implications for benefits management;
- Create the detailed business case and benefits management approach;
- Consult with project assurance whether the business case and benefits management approach meet the needs of the project board and corporate, programme management or customer;
- Update the relevant logs and registers if necessary;
- Seek approval from the project board.

15.4.7 Assemble the project initiation documentation

There needs to be a central point where all the information about the foundation of the project and its controls is gathered for agreement by the key stakeholders and for information and guidance for those involved in the project. The following actions are recommended:

- Carry out a cross-check on the information in the various management products to ensure their consistency;
- Consult with project assurance whether the assembled PID meets the needs of the project board and corporate, programme management or customer;
- Trigger the managing a stage boundary process to prepare for the first delivery stage and the end-stage report of the initiation stage;
- Request authorization from the project board to deliver the project.

15.5 Tailoring initiating a project

Simple project – The PID may be a single document. The risk, issue and quality register may be part of the same workbook in different tabs. The benefits management approach may be combined with the business case.

Agile project – During initiation it is decided what parts of the project will use agile. The product backlog (project product description) is established. The product owner (change authority) is assigned. The roadmap (project plan) is defined with the number of releases and timeboxes and with the size and composition of the development team(s).

The project product description may be more focused on the outcome, when the output will evolve during the project. The levels of uncertainty will determine the choice of agil techniques and the length of the timeboxes.

Commercial project – If an external supplier will be responsible for the total delivery o the project product, the initiating a project process is used by the external supplier to dra the quotation of the works based on the project initiation documentation established durin this process.

Project within a programme – Parts of the PID might be produced by a member of th programme team. The project's business case may be already included in the programme' business case. However the project manager has to ensure that a solid foundation for th project is established and that the project is desirable, viable and achievable.

Chapter 16
Controlling a stage

16.1 Purpose

The purpose of this process is to assign the work to be done, monitor the work, deal with issues, report on progress, and take corrective actions to ensure that the management stage remains within tolerance.

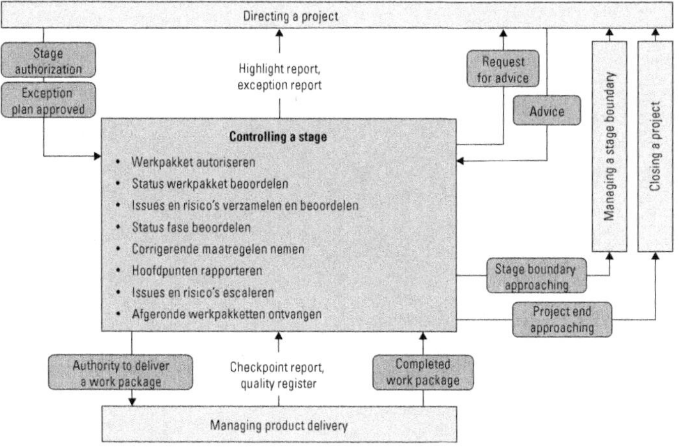

Figure 16.1 Controlling a stage process

16.2 Objective

The objective of the controlling a stage process is to ensure that:

- Attention is focused on the delivery of the management stage's products and uncontrolled change ('scope creep') is avoided;
- Risks and issues are kept under control;
- The business case is kept under review;

- The management stage's products are delivered within agreed tolerances, and that they support the achievement of the defined benefits.

16.3 Context

This process describes the project manager's day-to-day work during delivery. The process starts with the project board's authorization of the delivery of the management stage. Within this process the project manager triggers the managing product delivery process.

Towards the end of each intermediate stage the managing a stage boundary process is triggered. Towards the end of the last management stage the closing a project process is triggered, see figure 16.1.

For large or complex projects the controlling a stage process may also be used during initiation to control the work, where the initiating a project process may be short of guidance.

16.4 Activities

Controlling a stage consists of work package-related activities, monitoring and reporting related activities and issue/risk-related activities.

16.4.1 Authorize a work package

It is important that the work only commences and continues with the consent of the project manager. The vehicle for this is the work package. The following actions are recommended:

- Examine the current stage plan and understand the products, cost, effort and tolerances;
- Examine the PID to understand the required controls, quality standards and how the hand-over of products is to be carried out;
- Define the relevant work package;
- Review the work package with the team manager and make sure the team manager understands and accepts it and then authorize it;
- Review the team manager's team plan and update the stage plan for the timings;
- Update the quality register for planned quality activities and (if relevant) update the risk and issue register according to the relevant approaches;
- Update the configuration item records (if used).

16.4.2 Review work package status

A regular assessment of the work package is needed. The frequency of this is defined in the agreed work package. The following actions are recommended:

- Collect and review progress information from the checkpoint report that relates to the work package being executed;
- If necessary, update the risk and issue register;
- Update the stage plan for the current management stage with the actuals.

16.4.3 Receive completed work package

Once the work package is completed and approved, this should be confirmed. The following actions are recommended:

- Check that the team manager has completed the work, as defined in the work package, and that the quality register is complete;
- Ensure that each product in the work package is approved and that (if used) its configuration item record has been updated;
- Update the status of the work package in the stage plan as completed.

16.4.4 Capture and assess issues and risks

Issues and risks may be identified at any moment in time. These issues and risks should be registered in a consistent way before assessing their impact. The following actions are recommended:

- Register issues in the daily log, that can be dealt with informally and manage these issues from there;
- Capture and manage issues that need a more formal treatment, in accordance with the change control approach;
- Identify and manage risks in accordance with the risk management approach;
- If necessary take corrective action and ask for advice from the project board, or escalate the issue or risk and review the stage status.

16.4.5 Review the stage status

To prevent a management stage from getting out of control, a regular assessment of the progress is required. The following actions are recommended:

- Review progress of the management stage by reviewing checkpoint reports, forecast and actuals, quality issues, the risk register, the status of any corrective actions and the resource availability;
- Decide if any actions are required, for example authorizing a work package, reporting highlights, issues and risks escalation, taking corrective actions, asking the project board for advice, or logging any lessons. Another option might also be to continue as planned;
- Update stage plan, risk and issue register as necessary and review lessons;
- In the case of a phased handover, request a product status account for what is to be handed over. Make sure that these products have been approved by the appropriate people and meet the quality criteria and that operations and maintenance is ready to take over and hand over the products to the customer;
- If the end of an intermediate management stage is approaching trigger the managing a stage boundary process. If the end of the final management stage is approaching trigger the closing a project process.

16.4.6 Take corrective action

The objective of this activity is to resolve deviations from the stage plan within the agreed tolerances. Taking corrective action is usually triggered by reviewing the stage status. The following actions are recommended:

- Collect any relevant information about the deviation;
- Identify options to deal with a deviation and select the best option;
- Authorize or update a work package and – if needed - update the configuration item records of the products;
- Update the issue register and/or risk register with the change(s) resulting from the corrective action;
- Update the current stage plan with the actuals.

16.4.7 Escalate issues and risks

Issues and risks which are forecast to exceed the stage tolerances should be escalated to the project board. The following actions are recommended:

- Examine the stage plan and project plan and extrapolate what would happen if the deviation were allowed to continue;
- Define the options for recovery and assess them against the current stage plan, project plan and business case;

- Describe the situation, options and the recommended action(s) to the project board in an exception report (first oral, followed by a report).

16.4.8 Report highlights

The project manager has to inform the project board and other stakeholders about the progress of the management stage and project. The following actions are recommended:

- Assemble the necessary information from checkpoint reports, the risk, issue and quality register, the lessons log, the product status account and any revisions of the stage plan for the current reporting period;
- Review the corrective actions taken during the reporting period;
- Review the highlight report for the previous reporting period;
- Produce the highlight report for the current reporting period;
- Distribute the report to the project board and any other recipients as defined in the communication management approach.

16.5 Tailoring controlling a stage

Simple project – Where the project manager also fulfils the team manager's role, work packages should still be used to define and control the work of the individual team members. Highlight reports may be by e-mail or PowerPoint.

Agile project – When using agile, a collaborative style of managing is needed to keep the team empowered besides supporting a culture where change is embraced. Also take care that any tolerances should usually be only for scope and quality criteria, since time and money are fixed.

Work packages contain one or more timeboxes. The work for individual timeboxes are described by the product owner in sprint backlogs at the start of each timebox. Status updates are linked to the close-out at the end of the timebox. Intermediate updates can be taken from the information radiator.

Commercial project – Work package can take the form of a legally binding contract. Team plans may stay hidden if this is agreed in the contract. It is important to ensure that checkpoint reports contain enough information to control the work effectively and efficiently.

Project within a programme – Procedures for escalation should be aligned with th programme management strategies. Highlights reports also have to be sent to the programm office. The programme office also fulfils the assurance role from the programme perspective

Chapter 17
Managing product delivery

17.1 Purpose

The purpose of this process is to control the link between the project manager and the team manager(s), by placing formal requirements on accepting, executing and delivering project work.

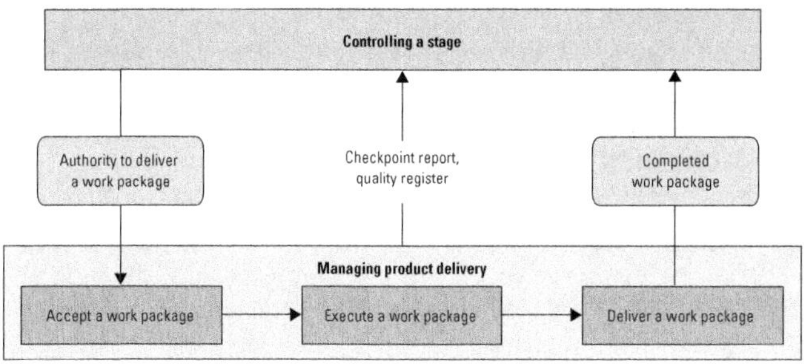

Figure 17.1 Managing product delivery process (based on: AXELOS Ltd.)

17.2 Objective

The objective of the managing product delivery process is to ensure that:

- Work allocated to the team is authorized and agreed;
- Those involved in a team are clear on the products to be delivered and the expected effort, cost and timescales;
- The planned products are delivered to expectations and within tolerance;
- Accurate progress information is provided to the project manager at an agreed frequency.

17.3 Context

This process is reviewing the project from the team manager's perspective, as shown in figure 17.1. This process is triggered by authorizing a work package by the project manager in the controlling a stage process. This process ends by accepance the completed work package b the project manager also in the controlling a stage process.

The team manager ensures that the work packages are executed and delivered by the team by

- Accepting and checking the authorized work package;
- Producing or updating the team plan for the assigned work packages. The team pla may have already been created by the team manager in parallel with the project manage creating the stage plan for the stage concerned in the managing a stage boundary process
- Ensuring that the products are delivered according to the agreed development method(s)
- Demonstrating that each product meets its quality criteria;
- Obtaining approval for completed products from the authorities identified in the relevan product descriptions;
- Delivering the products to the project manager according to any specified procedures ir the work package.

17.4 Activities

17.4.1 Accept a work package

The work allocated to the team should be agreed and authorized by the project manager. The following actions are recommended:

- Review the work package and clarify what is to be delivered, agree on constraints and tolerances. Understand the reporting requirements and how approval is obtained and how products are to be handed over, and confirm how the project manager will be informed about completion;
- Produce or update the team plan showing that the product(s) can be delivered within any given constraints;
- Seek advice from the supplier project assurance whether the team plan is viable and is in line with relevant supplier standards;
- Review any risks against the team plan and advise the project manager accordingly;
- Seek any necessary approval of the team plan;
- Consult with project assurance as to whether any extra reviewers are needed and update the quality register if applicable;
- Agree to deliver the work package.

It may be very effective to produce the team plan in parallel with the planning of the next stage plan by the project manager.

17.4.2 Execute a work package

During the executing of the work package, the team manager should make sure that the completed products are reviewed, report progress and raise risks and issues to the project manager if needed. The following actions are recommended:

- Manage the development of the deliverables effectively by addressing the agreed quality criteria, the required techniques, the agreed processes and procedures and the necessary interfaces;
- Monitor and control any issues, lessons and risks, and advise or notify the project manager accordingly;
- Obtain approval for the completed products, update the quality register and, if used, update the relevant configuration item records;
- Review the status of the work package products, report this to the project manager in checkpoint reports, update the team plan with the actuals and raise an issue when tolerances are forecast to be exceeded.

17.4.3 Deliver the work package

Notification of the completion of each work package should be passed through to the project manager. The following actions are recommended:

- Review the quality register and verify the completion of quality activities;
- Review the approval records to verify that all the agreed products are approved;
- Update the team plan with the actuals, deliver the products and notify the project manager of the work package's completion.

17.5 Tailoring managing product delivery

Simple project – For simple projects it may be sufficient that the team manager reports the checkpoints verbally and that the project records the progress in the daily log. If the project manager also takes on the role of team manager there is no need for formal checkpoint reports, as progress is then submitted by individual team members.

Agile project – The team manager (Scrum master) will have a facilitating role. The acceptance, execution and delivery of the work is done by the team itself. The team plan (timebox plan or sprint plan) is drafted by the team itself and agreed upon with the product owner. The performance of the works is monitored in daily stand-ups. Issues and risks that they cannot solve in time themselves, are raised by the team via the Scrum master to th project manager as impediments. The status of the work is made visible via an informatio radiator.

Commercial project – The work package is then part of the contractual agreement. Als the reporting and controlling activities in the managing product delivery process should b agreed upon as part of the contract. The supplier assurance should ensure the senior supplie that the team plans fit within the contractual conditions agreed.

Project within a programme – In most cases a programme does not have a direct link t the managing product delivery process. So the managing product delivery process is mostl free from any direct impact of the parent programme.

Chapter 18
Managing a stage boundary

18.1 Purpose

The purpose of this process is to enable the project manager to provide the project board with sufficient information so that it can review the success of the current stage, review the updated project plan and business case and approve the next stage plan or exception plan.

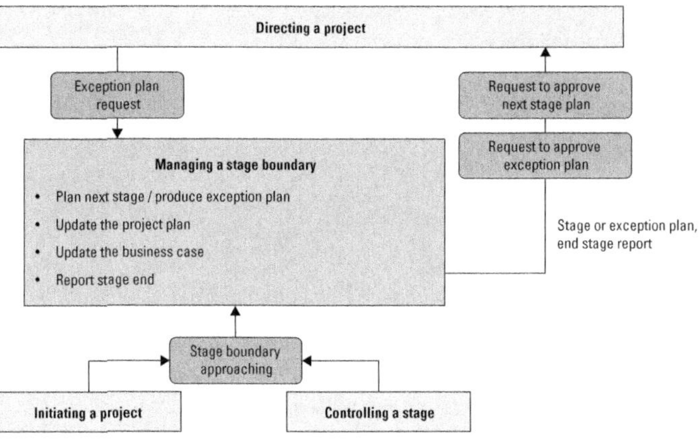

Figure 18.1 Managing a stage boundary process

18.2 Objective

The objective of the managing a stage boundary process is to:

- Assure the project board that the current management stage's products are complete and approved;
- Prepare the next stage plan or exception plan;
- Review and, if necessary, update the project initiation documentation;
- Provide the information needed for the project board to assess the continuing viability of the project;

- Record any lessons useful for coming stages or other projects;
- Request to approve the next stage plan or exception plan.

18.3 Context

This process is triggered by:

- The initiating a project process at the assemble the PID activity;
- The controlling a stage process when the stage boundary is approaching;
- The exception plan request by the project board in the directing a project process.

At the end of the initiation stage the managing a stage boundary process is limited to plan the first delivery stage and report the stage end activities.

The process ends with a request by the project manager to the project board to approve the next stage plan or exception plan, see figure 18.1.

18.4 Activities

18.4.1 Plan the next stage

Near the end of the current management stage the project manager produces the next stage plan, after consultation with project board, project assurance, team managers and other stakeholders. When preparing the last stage plan, the activities to close the project should be included in the next stage plan as well. The following actions are recommended:

- Review the PID regarding any required changes;
- Produce the stage plan for the next management stage, including a review of the project plan, the quality management approach and the risk and issue register for issues and risks that may affect the next stage;
- Create or update the product breakdown structure, product descriptions and product flow diagram for the next management stage;
- Update the issue and risk register as necessary;
- Update the quality register for planned quality management activities;
- Create or update the configuration item records, if used, for the relevant products to be delivered.

18.4.2 Update the project plan

The project plan has to be updated with actuals from the current management stage and with a forecast of the next management stage. The following actions are recommended:

- Check if the current stage plan is up-to-date;
- Revise the project plan to incorporate current stage actuals, the next stage forecasts, any changes to the project product description, any implication of issues and risks, any modified or additional products demanded by the project board and any changes within the project initiation documentation;
- Update the issue and risk register as necessary.

18.4.3 Update the business case

Before authorizing the next stage plan or exception plan the project board has to convince itself that the project is still desirable, viable and achievable. Therefore there is a need to update the business case when new insights into costs and end dates have been established. The following actions are recommended:

- Examine the project plan to see whether project end dates or costs have changed and might, therefore, influence the cost/benefit analysis;
- Examine and review the impact of approved changes and other issues that might affect the benefits;
- Assess the key risks that may affect the business case. Assess the aggregated risk exposure to remain within the risk tolerances. Check whether risk tolerances need to be redefined;
- Update the benefits management approach with the results from any benefit management action undertaken during the current stage;
- Revise business case and benefits management approach and update the issue and risk register as necessary.

18.4.4 Report stage end

This activity should take place as close as possible to the management stage end. This activity also may be required if the project board requests the project manager to produce an exception plan in response to an exception report. The following actions are recommended:

- Review the status of the updated business case, the stage plan, the team performance, the product performance and the raised issues and risks;
- Prepare the end stage report, and check the communication management approach for external interested parties that need a copy of it.

18.4.5 Produce an exception plan

This activity is triggered by the request of the project board to produce such a plan in the directing a project process. Exception plans are requested by the project board in response to an exception report raised by the project manager. The following actions are recommended

- Review the PID regarding any required changes. Update the PID as necessary;
- Produce the exception plan;
- Examine the stage plan to define the products to be produced;
- Examine the exception report for details on e.g. recommended actions;
- Examine the quality management approach if new products need to be produced;
- Update the product breakdown structure, product descriptions and product flow diagram relating to this exception plan;
- Update the issue and risk register as necessary;
- Update the quality register for planned quality management activities;
- Create or update the configuration item records – if used - for the relevant products to be delivered.

18.5 Tailoring managing a stage boundary

Simple project – In a simple project there usually is only one delivery stage. The managing a stage boundary process will then only be used at the end of the initiation stage to produce the end stage report and the stage plan for the delivery stage or at the request of the project board to produce an exception plan. If there is only one delivery stage, the stage plan can be incorporated in the project plan if the project plan covers the appropriate detail.

Agile project – When using an agile approach the end of a release may mark the end of a management stage. The managing a stage boundary process would mean a confirmation of the results at the end of the management stage, an assessment of the ongoing viability of the project as a whole and a prioritizing of the high-level features that must be realized during the next management stage.

Commercial project – If the entire project product is subcontracted to an external party, then during the managing a stage boundary processes the subsequent stage contracts are defined within the framework contract to deliver the project product.

Project within a programme – When the project is within a programme, the project stage boundaries should be aligned with the management stage gates.

Chapter 19
Closing a project

19.1 Purpose

The purpose of this process is to provide a point at which acceptance for the project product is confirmed, and to verify that the objectives in the original PID, and its subsequently approved changes, have been achieved, or that the project has nothing more to contribute.

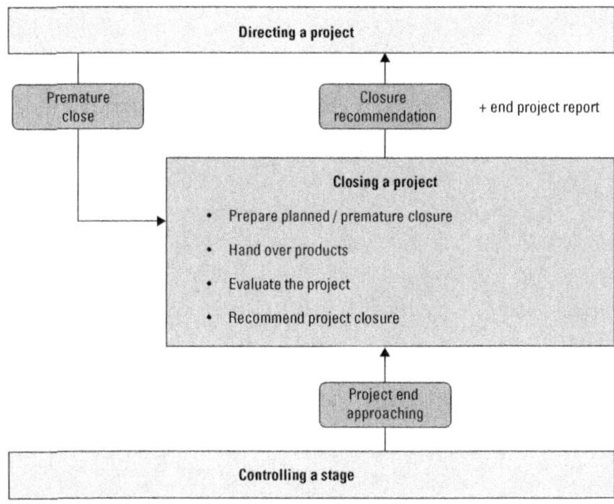

Figure 19.1 Closing a project process

19.2 Objective

The objective is of the closing a project process is to:

- Verify the user acceptance of the project product;
- Ensure that the host site is able to support the products;
- Review the project's performance against its baselines;
- Assess any benefits that have been realized and update the benefits management approach;
- Provide follow-on action recommendations that address all unresolved issues and risks.

19.3 Context

A clear end to a project is always better than a slow drift into operational use as it transfer ownership from the project management team to the customer and subsequently ends th project management team's responsibilities and project costs no longer occur.

The closing a project process is triggered by the controlling a stage process when the end o the final management stage is approaching and by the directing a project process when the project board requests a premature closure, see figure 19.1.

19.4 Activities

19.4 1 Prepare planned closure

Before recommending closure, the project manager must ensure that the expected results have all been achieved and delivered. The following actions are recommended:

- Update the project plan with the latest actuals;
- Request a product status account from project support and confirm that the project has delivered the project product as agreed and that the acceptance criteria have been met;
- Get approval to notify corporate, programme management or customer that resources can be released.

19.4.2 Prepare premature closure

In situations where the project board instructs the project manager to close the project prematurely, the project manager should ensure that work is not simply abandoned but that the project recovers anything that might be of value, and any gaps that might be due to the project's premature closure are raised with corporate, programme management or customer. The following actions are recommended:

- Update the issue register by recording the issue of the premature closure;
- Update the project plan with the latest actuals;
- Request a product status account from project support and determine the status of the project product's components;
- Agree upon the means for recovering completed products or products in progress. This can include additional work to create, secure or finish products that may be useful to other projects;

- Seek approval to give notice to corporate, programme management or customer that resources can be released early.

19.4.3 Hand over products

The project product is handed over to the operation and maintenance before the project can be closed. This can either happen at the end of the project in a single release, or in a phased delivery with a number of releases. The following actions are recommended:

- Examine the change control approach to confirm how products have to be handed over to the customer;
- Confirm that the operational and maintenance environment is in place;
- Confirm user, operational and maintenance acceptance;
- Ensure that the project product is handed over to the customer;
- Update the relevant configuration item records, if used;
- Prepare follow-on action recommendations for the project product including uncompleted work, issues and risks;
- Update the benefits management approach with the results of the benefits reviews taken and the post-project benefits reviews planned.

19.4.4 Evaluate the project

Successful organizations learn from their project experiences. Therefore there is a need to assess how (un)successful the project has been and what improved estimates might be of help to future projects. The following actions are recommended:

- Review the original intent of the PID and the approved changes as defined by the current PID and prepare the end project report;
- Update the business case with the project actuals and the benefits realized so far;
- Prepare a lessons report and include it in the end project report with lessons that can be useful for future projects.

19.4.5 Recommend project closure

A closure recommendation should be raised to the project board, once the project manager is certain that the project can be closed. The following actions are recommended:

- Check the communication management approach for relevant stakeholders and for communication activities at this point;

- Tidy up and archive project information to permit a future audit of the performance actions and decisions of the project management team;
- Prepare and send a project closure notification to the project board, stating that th project has closed.

19.5 Tailoring closing a project

Simple projects – In a simple project all the closing a project activities may take place in a single meeting. The handing over of the project product may not need to be formally documented.

Agile project – When using an agile approach the handover of the individual products and features takes place at the end of the various timeboxes and/or releases. Therefore the closing a project process can be shortened in time and effort.

Commercial project – In commercial projects a separate maintenance and/or warranty period may be part of the project contract after handing over the project product.

Project within a programme – When the project is within a programme, the reviewing and realizing of the benefits is part of the programme.

PART IV TAILORING AND ADOPTING

Chapter 20
Introduction tailoring and adopting PRINCE2

The seventh PRINCE2 principle requires that PRINCE2 should be tailored for the particular circumstances of the project. If PRINCE2 is not tailored it is unlikely that the project management approach will suit the project's need.

Tailoring can be done in two different ways: Tailoring PRINCE2 directly for an individual project (adapting) and the tailoring of the organization's project management standard; the adopting of PRINCE2 in an organization.

20.1 Tailoring PRINCE2

Tailoring PRINCE2 for an individual project consists of the adaptation of e.g. the themes and processes to suit specific circumstances. Examples in this area are defining project specific responsibilities, adjusting or combining part of the management products and customize the processes so they are fit for the specific project.

20.2 Adopting PRINCE2

When projects are managed regularly in an organization, it makes sense to adopt PRINCE2 as the standard project management method. Such a standardized approach can be customized to suit the organization's internal processes and procedures and to suit the characteristics of the projects that are executed in that organization. Usually this standard may consist of techniques and tools to support the project management.

Table 20.01 describes the main focus areas of tailoring PRINCE2 to a specific project and adopting PRINCE2 as the standard in an organization.

Table 20.01 Tailoring and adopting PRINCE2

Tailoring to a project	**Quality assurance**
Tailoring PRINCE2 for an individual project to suit specific circumstances. **Focus on:** • Adapt themes through approaches and controls • Incorporate specific terms/language • Revise product descriptions for the management products • Revise role descriptions • Adjust processes By the project manager	Adopting PRINCE2 as the standard project management method in an organization. **Focus on:** • Adjust to rules and regulations • Integrate with business processes • Assure processes and procedures • Scale rules and guidance • Prescribe templates and definitions • Prescribe techniques, tools and applications to use • Provide training and development By the process owner or process manager

Chapter 21
Tailoring PRINCE2

The purpose of tailoring PRINCE2 to the specific project is to suit the project management to the characteristics and the circumstances of the project. This improves the method's effectiveness and prevents unnecessary bureaucracy.
If the organization does not have its own project management method (yet), then tailoring will be done to suit the needs of the project directly. If the organization has its own PRINCE2 based method, then this embedded method should be tailored to the specific project.

21.1 Elements to tailor

PRINCE2 aspects that may be tailored:

- **Processes** – can be combined or adjusted, but they cannot be omitted;
- **Themes** – can be more or less applied, often using techniques appropriate to the project;
- **Roles** – will be fulfilled by specific persons. Roles can be split up, or combined as long as there are no conflicts of interest;
- **Management products** – may be combined or split up as well to suit the specific needs of the project. Some management products may be omitted when there is no need for them to control the project;
- **Terminology** – can be adjusted to the specific terminology of the organization as long as this is done consistently.

The PRINCE2 principles cannot be tailored as they are universal and always apply. If an organization omits one of these principles, it cannot be called a PRINCE2 project.

The way to tailor PRINCE2 to the project depends on the characteristic and the context of the project. Of importance are the size and the complexity of the project, whether the project will be run using waterfall or agile, whether the project is run with external parties and whether a project is run as a stand-alone project or within a programme or portfolio.

It is the project manager's responsibility to tailor the project. The way the project will tail PRINCE2 is established as part of the PID, and therefore subject to the project boar approval.

21.2 Scaling projects

The ways to manage the project depends, among other things on the size, complexit importance, visibility and the amount of risk, see table 21.1.

Table 21.1 Projects with varying complexity

Complexity	Characteristics	Applying PRINCE2
High ↑	**Programme:** • Business transformation	• This is **not** a project • Managing Successful Programmes
	Highly complex project: • Very risky, high costs • Very important and visible • Multiple parties and organizations involved • International	• Multiple delivery stages • Extended project board • Separate team managers and project support • Individual management products
	Normal project: • Risk, costs, importance and visibility are at medium level. • Customer or supplier is external • Several locations or sites	• One or more delivery stages • Standard project board • Separate team managers and project support are optional • Some management products are combined
	Simple project: • Risk, costs, importance and visibility are low • One organization involved • One location or site	• One delivery stage • Simple project board • One team; no separate team managers and project support • Combined management products
↓ Low	**Task:** • Within business as usual. • Funding from operational budgets. • Direct justification	• This is **not** a project. • No project board. • Combining starting up and initiating the project. • Project manager will also carry out specialist work.

Business transformations can be best managed as a programme using the method Managing Successful Programmes (MSP). Assignments within business as usual can be best managed as a task.

The use of PRINCE2 generally decreases the amount of risk associated with the project.

On the other hand, when the tailoring does not suit the need of the project, the amount of risk will increase.

21.3 Small projects

Small projects have mostly one delivery stage. When managing a simple and small project, the processes starting up a project and initiating a project may be combined, see figure 21.01. At very simple projects, the starting up and initiating a project processes can even be accomplished in one single conversation.

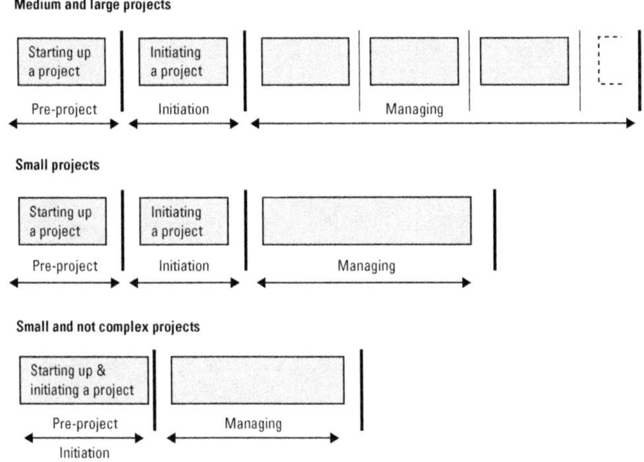

Figure 21.01 various stages in projects

PRINCE2 is supported by a large number of management products. If in a small project the use of all of these management products are described, this project will suffer more than benefit from this. In situations such as these, in the majority of cases it is the method that is to be blamed and not the use of it, however unfair that may seem. Therefore tailoring PRINCE2 is important, especially for small projects.

Small projects usually consist of only one delivery team whereby the project manager is also responsible for carrying out a part of the specialist works. A risk in this situation is that the project manager interferes too much with the work of the team member(s) with the effect of team members not taking full responsibility. This happens especially when the team member(s) has the right amount of expertise but not the right amount of delegated responsibility.

21.4 Agile projects

In agile projects empowered teams produce shippable products in timeboxes with customer satisfaction as the highest priority. Such projects value individuals over processes, working deliverables over comprehensive documentation and responding to change over following a plan. At the end of each timebox a retrospective is held to review the team performance during this last timebox.

This complies totally to the PRINCE2 principles of continued business justification, manage by stages, learn from experience, manage by exception, focus on products and tailor to suit the project.

Continued business justification states that the value for the customer is the leading principle for every project. Learn from experience emphasizes that evaluating should not take place only at the end of the project but at every milestone. Manage by exception consists of delegating enough responsibility to the lower level so that they can work self-organized. Focus on products means that the focus is on the products to realize instead of activities. Tailor to suit the project emphasizes that among others that the amount of documentation should depend on the project approach.

21.5 Commercial projects

In a commercial environment third parties can deliver individual work packages but also be responsible for the total delivery of the project product.

In this last situation we can distinguish two situations. One possibility is that the supplier based on the project brief, drafts first a quotation for delivering the PID and subsequently the supplier based on the PID, drafts the quotation for the delivering of the project product. In this situation the PRINCE2 processes are followed in full.

Another possibility is when the supplier is asked to draft a quotation for the delivering of the project product straight away. Then the process starting up a project is carried out by the supplier internally to review the request for quotation, to decide whether to make the offer and to plan how to draft the actual quotation. Subsequently the supplier then drafts in the process initiating the project the actual quotation.

In commercial projects special attention should be given to the management approaches, as they should be aligned with the contract between the customer and the supplier.

21.6 Projects within a programme

A programme is a temporary organization created to coordinate, direct and oversee the implementation of a set of related projects and activities in order to deliver outcomes and benefits related to the organization's strategic objectives.

The projects' deliverables are the means with which the organization units should create the desired outcome and realize the benefits. The focal point is the organization and its organizational units, that have a demand and must ensure that the changes will be executed and the benefits realized.

The programme board consists of the programme sponsor, the programme manager and the respective business change managers. The business change manager is responsible for creating the desired outcome and to realize the resulting benefits within his organizational unit. This responsibility makes him the ideal senior user in the project that delivers the necessary output to create the desired outcome.

When the project is within a programme, the project brief might be created by the programme. Still the project manager has to assess this brief to ensure that the project brief is consistent and realistic.

Also the project business case may already been created by the programme. The benefits management approach may e part of the programme benefits realization plan. The other management approaches may also have the programme management approach as reference.

When creating the project plan, the dependencies with programme activities and other projects of the programme should be shown. The programme defines the project tolerances and the number and length of the management stages. When there is a forecast that the project plan will exceed its tolerances, this should be escalated to the programme level.

21.7 Multi-organizational projects

When two or more independent organizations initiate a project together, the ownership is shared by these organizations. In such circumstances it is advised to organize it as programme and to appoint one representative of that programme as the one and only executive of that project.

Chapter 22
Adopting PRINCE2

In organizations with many projects, it may be less effective and efficient to ask each project manager to tailor PRINCE2 directly for each individual project. Then it makes sense to develop their own project management method based on PRINCE2 customized to their needs and circumstances.

Adopting PRINCE2 then consists of two main activities:
- Tailoring PRINCE2 to create their own project management method;
- Embedding this tailored method by making sure that people understand it and use it wisely.

22.1 Tailoring to create its own method

Tailoring PRINCE2 to suit the needs of the project is done for an individual project. Tailoring to create the organization's own project management method is to adjust the PRINCE2 method to the characteristics and the circumstances of the projects undertaken by the organization, reckoning with the internal and external policies, procedures and practices.

This own method may be documented in a project management handbook that can act as a dynamic document that captures the latest practices and lessons learnt. It is essential that such a standard is understood and put into practice by all parties concerned. Training and coaching is important to create an organization-wide acceptance.

When an organization wants to create a customized project management standard, the people need to know why this is necessary and what the management wants to achieve with it. Is there a need to improve efficiency, or to manage risks more effectively, or because our customers would like that we work more consistently? Understanding the outcome by all parties involved creates buy-in, improves decision-making and ensures a method that suits the needs of the organization.

Themes, processes, roles, management products and terminology are customized to ensure outcomes can be realized. Principles are not tailored, as they are universal and always apply.

Themes – The PRINCE2 themes will be tailored to suit the existing practices, guidelines and regulations. The handbook should give guidelines on how to use the themes e.g. when using a waterfall model or an agile framework. Specific steps in the staging of the various projects can be added to support the project managers, as well as specific techniques and applications.

Processes – When adjusting the PRINCE2 processes it is not advisable to omit processes or activities within them. Tailoring processes is more about to what extent and in what degree of formality the process will be used, instead of omitting processes or activities.

Roles – It is more important that roles and responsibilities are clearly understood by all parties involved and acted upon, than that there is a signed role description. Sometimes signed agreements are of course very helpful, but not all circumstances will benefit from full formality.

Terminology – A consistent terminology will improve communication between parties in general. However using the same terminology does not necessarily mean we have to use PRINCE2 terminology strictly as described in the method. Using a project charter instead of project brief or project contract instead of PID, when this was already common language, can support a wider acceptance.

Management products – Furthermore for management products it may be wise to partly retain the existing templates and to adjust these based on the PRINCE2 composition. Make sure that all elements of the PRINCE2 management products are incorporated in these templates. Only if there is an valid reason to omit certain elements, those parts can be left out.

Tailoring to suit the needs of the individual project – Also, an own project management method should be tailored to the needs of the individual projects. There is no one size fits all. Therefore in the organization's project management handbook guidelines should be included on how to tailor the standard to the needs of the individual projects. Especially for simple projects an overkill of tools and templates should be prevented.

22.2 Embedding PRINCE2

When introducing its own project management method, just publishing the handbook is not enough. People should change the way they work. Cultural and behavioral aspects should be aken into account. This cannot be done via a project. Such a change should be undertaken s a programme.

All stakeholders should be involved: project managers, team managers, project members, project support, project assurance, executives, line managers and the senior management. Ask them for advice and let them review the deliverables. Since one cannot involve every individual, make use of 'key users' or 'ambassadors' This ensures a qualified output/outcome and a widespread acceptance among (future) users.

Acceptance and support from the individuals who should change their way of working is essential. To get their support and acceptance it must be certain that:

- The need to change is clear;
- There is support from the top of the organization;
- The future state is visualized and understood;
- It is clear what changes are needed to achieve this future state;
- Those who are affected by the change are engaged;
- Necessary capabilities are developed and obstacles are removed;
- Short-term wins are created and celebrated and gains are consolidated.

A proven approach is to create a group of acknowledged project experts that share their lessons and best practices in regular sessions, thus creating a consistent and agreed new way of working, ready for inclusion in the project management handbook. Ideally these experts sessions are led and facilitated by a recognized expert in the field, who due to his experience may propose solutions the group may never have thought of.

After the initial introduction it is not enough to only train the relevant people. People should keep improving themselves by organizing counseling, peer-to-peer review and coaching. Communication is also needed to keep the urgency and the benefits for the new way of working understood. And keep in mind that 'what we pay attention to grows', there should be regular reviews to monitor the progress towards objectives and if necessary to direct the change in the desired way. Provide stakeholders with clear and regular updates.

Implementation in incremental steps is one of the most practical and effective ways to proceed. By learning form experience the desired change can evolve in time and offers the right amount of flexibility to direct the change initiative.

To consolidate the gains it is essential that there is a sponsor at senior management leve Further create a center of excellence, directed by the sponsor, to develop and maintain th new way of working. Set up a website explaining the new method, with the templates to b used, but also with lessons and success stories about the use of the new method.

Make sure that experienced and senior experts are appointed as owner of relevant part of the new method, like risk management or quality control. Create one or more projec management communities that capture and share lessons learned. Assess the effectiveness o the new method regularly. For the latter a maturity assessment can be used.

22.2 Maturity assessment

A maturity assessment is an assessment of the organizational capability in a given area o skill. The maturity model that is aligned with PRINCE2 is P3M3. P3M3 is a maturity mode for project, programme and portfolio management and measures the maturity of each o these perspectives as well as the integral maturity where the three perspectives are combined

P3M3 defines five maturity levels, see figure 22.01:

1. **Awareness** – No formal standards. Success is dependent on people's individual competences
2. **Repeatable** – There is a some form of standard practice in individual projects;
3. **Defined** – There is one generally adopted method for the organization;
4. **Managed** – The effectiveness of the method is measured and managed;
5. **Optimized** – An organization capable of continuous improvement.

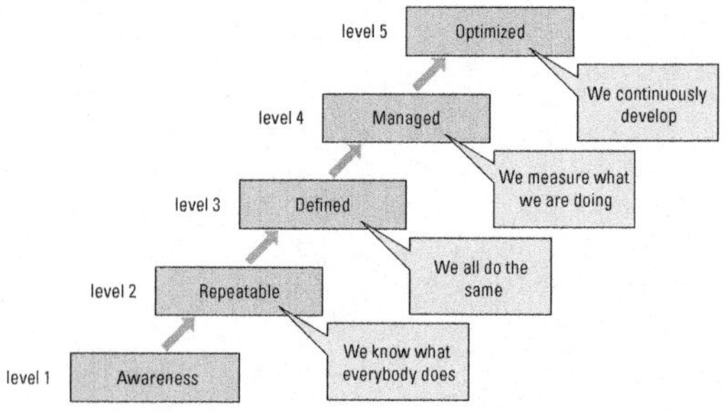

Figure 22.01 P3M3 maturity levels

An organization that has a well-defined project management method, based on PRINCE2, would become at least a maturity level 3 organization.

Appendix A
Outline product descriptions management products

Management products should be tailored to the needs of the project and its environment. Management products may be text documents, slides, spreadsheets, wall charts or information on screen.

Some management products may not be used in all projects. Management products may also be combined when they fulfill related purposes.

PRINCE2 do not recommend the composition of the configuration item record, the daily log, the lesson report and the product status account.

PRINCE2 distinguishes baselines, records and reports, see figure A.1.

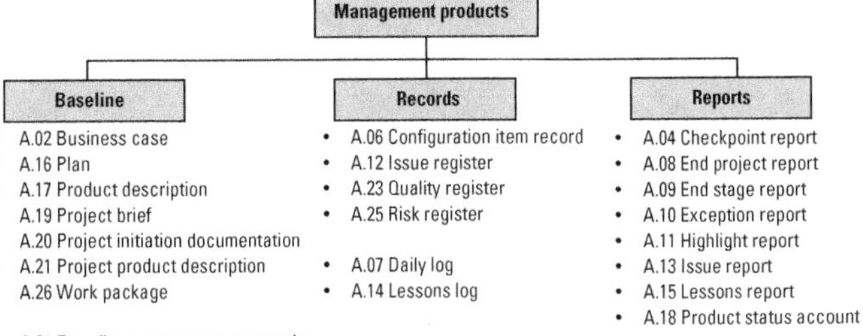

Figure A.1 Overview management products

A.1 Benefits management approach

The benefits management approach defines the benefits management actions that must b put in place to ensure that the project's outcomes are achieved and to confirm that th project's benefits are realized (benefits reviews).

Composition

- What benefits are to be measured and managed;
- Who is accountable for the expected benefits;
- How and when can the outcomes and benefits be achieved/measured;
- What resources are needed;
- Baselines measures;
- How the performance of the project product will be reviewed.

A.2 Business case

The business case documents the justification for undertaking the project against which continuing viability is tested.

Composition

- Executive summary;
- Reasons;
- Business options;
- Expected benefits and their tolerances;
- Expected dis-benefits;
- Timescale;
- Costs;
- Investment appraisal;
- Major risks.

A.3 Change control approach

The change control approach is used to identify, assess and control changes to the baseline and to protect the project's products. It describes how, when and by whom an effective issue management and change control procedure is achieved.

Composition

- Introduction;
- Issue management and change control procedure (including capturing, assessing, proposing actions, deciding and implementing activities);
- Tools and techniques;
- Definition of the content of the issue register;
- Composition of the issue report;
- Timing of issue management and change control activities;
- Roles and responsibilities;
- Scales for priority and severity: priority for requests for change and off-specifications and severity, in terms of the level of management that can decide on the issue.

A.4 Checkpoint report

A checkpoint report is used by the team manager to report on the status of the work package to the project manager at a frequency that is defined in the work package.

Composition

- Date;
- Period;
- Follow-ups;
- This reporting period, covering products completed and being developed, quality management activities and lessons identified;
- The next reporting period, covering products to be developed and completed, and quality management activities;
- Status of the work package tolerance;
- Issues and risks.

A.5 Communication management approach

The communication management approach describes the frequency and means of communication to all parties involved. It facilitates stakeholder engagement and a bidirectional and controlled communication.

Composition

- Introduction;
- Communication procedure;

- Tools and techniques;
- Records;
- Reporting;
- Timing of communication activities;
- Roles and responsibilities;
- Stakeholder analysis:
  - Identification of each interested party;
  - Current relationship;
  - Desired relationship;
  - Interfaces;
  - Key messages;
- Information needs of each interested party:
  - Information required to be provided from the project;
  - Information required to be provided to the project;
  - Information provider and recipient;
  - Frequency, means and format of communication.

A.6 Configuration item record

A configuration item record records relevant information about a product such as history status and version and any details of important relationships between them. Whether it is actually used is defined in the change control approach.

The composition of a configuration item record is not defined by PRINCE2.

A.7 Daily log

The daily log records informal issues, actions and events not covered by any other register, log or report. It is the project manager's diary. It is also used as a repository for issues and risks during the starting up a project process when the registers have not been created yet.

The composition of the daily log is not defined by PRINCE2.

A.8 End project report

The end project report confirms the handover of all products and provides an updated business case and an assessment of how well the project has done against the original

PID. The end project report may also include the lesson report and the follow-on action recommendations.

Composition

- Project manager's report on the project's performance;
- Review of the business case;
- Review of the project objectives;
- Review of team performance;
- Review of:
  - Quality records;
  - Approval records;
  - Off-specifications;
  - Project product handover;
  - Summary of follow-on action recommendations;
- Lessons.

A.9 End stage report

An end stage report summarizes the actual progress, the overall project situation and the performance during the last management stage at the end of each intermediate management stage. The project board uses the end stage report in tandem with the next stage plan to decide if and how to continue with the project.

Composition

- Project manager's report on the management stage's performance;
- Review of the business case;
- Review of project and management stage objectives;
- Review of team performance;
- Review of:
  - Quality records;
  - Approval records;
  - Off-specifications;
  - Phased handover (if applicable);
  - Summary of follow-on action recommendations (if applicable);
- Lessons;
- Summary of the current risks and issues;
- Forecast for project and next management stage.

A.10 Exception report

An exception report is produced by the project manager when a stage plan or project pla is forecast to exceed its tolerance levels. It offers the project board information about th exception, its impact, the options and the recommendations on how to proceed.

Composition

- Exception title;
- Cause of the exception;
- Consequences of the deviation for the project and/or corporate, programm management and the customer;
- Options and the effect of each option on the business case, risks and tolerances;
- Recommendation(s);
- Lessons.

A.11 Highlight report

A highlight report is produced by the project manager to inform the project board and other stakeholders, providing a summary of the status of a stage at a defined frequency. The project board uses it to monitor progress of the project and management stage.

Composition

- Date;
- Period;
- Management stage status summary;
- This reporting period, covering the status of work packages, products completed, products planned but not started or not completed in the period, and any corrective actions;
- The next reporting period, covering the status of work packages, products to be completed and any corrective actions to be finished;
- Project and management stage tolerance status;
- Requests for change;
- Key issues and risks;
- Lessons.

A.12 Issue register

The issue register contains information about all issues that are being managed formally. The project manager should monitor it on a regular basis.

Composition

Each record in the issue register should contain:

- Issue identifier;
- Issue type (request for change, off-specification or problem/concern);
- Date raised;
- Raised by;
- Issue report author;
- Issue description (with cause and effect);
- Priority and severity;
- Status;
- Closure date.

A.13 Issue report

An issue report contains the description, impact assessment and recommendations for each formal issue. The issue report is created and updated during the steps of the issue and change control procedure.

Composition

- Issue identifier (reference to issue register);
- Issue type (request for change, off-specification or problem/concern);
- Date raised;
- Raised by;
- Issue report author;
- Issue description (with cause and effect);
- Impact analysis;
- Recommendation;
- Priority and severity;
- Decision;
- Approved by;
- Decision date;
- Closure date.

A.14 Lessons log

The lessons log is a repository for lessons (both good and bad experiences) that can b applied to this project or future projects. Some lessons originate from previous project whilst other lessons originate from within the current project.

Composition

- Lesson type (useful for this project only and/or also for future projects);
- Lesson detail (event, effect, cause or trigger, early warning indicators, whether it wa previously identified as a risk, recommendations);
- Date logged;
- Logged by;
- Priority.

A.15 Lessons report

A lessons report is used to pass on any lessons to corporate or programme management o customer. A lessons report may be created at any time and may be included in the end stag report or end project report.

The composition of the lessons report is not defined by PRINCE2.

A.16 Plan

A plan is a statement of how, when and by whom objectives are to be achieved. It shows therefore the major products, activities and resources needed. A plan should not only cover activities to create products, but also to manage product creation.

Composition

- Plan description (plan level and planning approach);
- Plan prerequisites;
- External dependencies;
- Planning assumptions;
- Delivery approaches;
- Lessons incorporated;
- Monitoring and control;
- Budgets (time, cost and provisions for risks and changes);

- Tolerances (on time, cost and scope);
- Product descriptions;
- Schedule with graphical representation of:
  - Gantt or bar chart;
  - Product breakdown structure and product flow diagram;
  - Activity network;
  - Table of resources required by resource type;
  - Table of requested/assigned specific resources by name.

In the project plan the project product description is included.

A.17 Product description

A product description describes all relevant aspects of the product such as its sources, quality criteria, quality methods and quality skills required.

Composition

- Identifier;
- Title;
- Purpose that the product will fulfil;
- Composition;
- Derivation (source products);
- Format and presentation (characteristics and appearance);
- Development skills required;
- Quality criteria;
- Quality tolerance (range to be acceptable);
- Quality method;
- Quality skills required;
- Quality responsibilities.

A.18 Product status account

A product status account summarizes the status of products under change control. This account can be useful when confirmation of the version number of products is required.

The composition of the product status account is not defined by PRINCE2.

A.19 Project brief

The project brief describes all relevant aspects of the project to ensure that the prerequisite for initiating a project are in place.

Composition

- Project definition, which includes:
  - Background;
  - Project objectives (time, cost, quality, scope, risk and benefits);
  - Desired outcomes;
  - Project scope and exclusions;
  - Constraints and assumptions;
  - Project tolerances;
  - The user(s) and any other known interested parties;
  - Interfaces and prerequisites project delivery;
- Outline business case (reasons why and the selected business option);
- Project product description;
- Project approach;
- Project management team structure and role descriptions;
- References.

A.20 Project initiation documentation (PID)

The PID is a set of documents that brings together the key information needed (1) to ensure there is a sound basis before asking the project board to make any significant commitment to the project; (2) to act as a base document against which progress, issues and viability can be assessed; (3) to provide a single source of reference for staff joining the project organization.

Composition

- Project definition, which includes:
  - Background;
  - Project objectives and desired outcomes;
  - Project scope and exclusions;
  - Constraints and assumptions;
  - The user(s) and any other known interested parties;

  - o Interfaces;
  - o Project approach;
- Business case;
- Project management team structure and role descriptions;
- Quality management approach;
- Change control approach;
- Risk management approach;
- Communication management approach;
- Project plan;
- Project controls;
- Tailoring of PRINCE2.

The benefits management approach is no part of the PID!

A.21 Project product description

The project product description is the product description of the project product to gain agreement from the users and operations and maintenance on the project's output. At the end of the project it is used to check whether the project has delivered what was expected.

Composition

- Title;
- Purpose of the project product;
- Composition (major products);
- Derivation (source products);
- Development skills required;
- Customer's quality expectations;
- Acceptance criteria;
- Project-level quality tolerances;
- Acceptance method;
- Acceptance responsibilities.

A.22 Quality management approach

The quality management approach describes the techniques, standards, processes, procedures and responsibilities to be applied in the project, to define how quality will be managed.

Composition

- Introduction;
- Quality management procedure:
  - Project assurance and quality assurance;
  - Quality planning and quality control;
- Tools and techniques;
- Records (format and composition of e.g. the quality register);
- Reporting (their purpose, composition, timing and recipients);
- Timing of quality management activities;
- Roles and responsibilities.

A.23 Quality register

The quality register captures summary details of all planned and executed quality management activities and is a pointer to the quality records.

Composition

Each record in the quality register should include:

- Quality identifier;
- Product identifier(s);
- Product title(s);
- Method;
- Roles and responsibilities;
- Planned, forecast and actual dates for quality activities and sign-off;
- Result of the quality activities (e.g. fail or pass);
- Reference to quality records.

A.24 Risk management approach

The risk management approach describes the techniques, standards, processes, procedures and responsibilities to be applied in the project, to define how risks will be managed.

Composition

- Introduction;
- Risk management process or procedure (if this varies from the corporate, programme management or customer standards, the variance should be justified);

- Tools and techniques;
- Records (format and composition of e.g. the risk register);
- Reporting (their purpose, composition, timing and recipients);
- Timing of risk management activities;
- Roles and responsibilities;
- Scales (for estimating probability and impact);
- Proximity (e.g. imminent, current stage, this project, after the project);
- Risk categories and risk response categories;
- Early-warning indicators;
- Risk tolerance;
- Risk budget.

A.25 Risk register

The risk register captures summary details of all the identified risks related to the project.

Composition

Each record in the risk register should include:

- Risk identifier;
- Risk author;
- Date registered;
- Risk category;
- Risk description (cause, event and effect);
- Probability, impact and expected value;
- Proximity;
- Risk response categories;
- Risk response;
- Risk status;
- Risk owner;
- Risk actionee.

A.26 Work package

A work package describes the information relevant to the creation, management and handing over of one or more products.

Composition

The content may vary depending on the project:

- Date;
- Team manager or person authorized;
- Work package description;
- Techniques, processes and procedures to use;
- Development interfaces;
- Operations and maintenance interfaces;
- Change control requirements;
- Joint agreements (on effort, cost, time, dates and key milestones);
- Tolerances (cost, time, scope, quality and risk);
- Constraints;
- Reporting arrangements;
- Problem handling and escalation;
- Extracts from or reference to stage plan and product descriptions;
- Approval method.

Appendix B
Roles and responsibilities

B.1 Project board

The project board is accountable for the success of the project and directs the project within the delegated boundaries set by corporate, programme management or customer. The project board is responsible for the communication between the project and external stakeholders. Members of the project board may delegate some responsibilities to project assurance and change authority.

Derived from this, the project board will:

- Confirm project tolerances with corporate, programme management or customer;
- Approve the project brief and initiation stage plan and authorize the initiation of the project;
- Approve the PID and the first stage plan and authorize the project;
- Decide whether to delegate the project assurance and change authority;
- Set stage tolerances and scales for severity and priority for issues and risks;
- Approve the next stage plan or exception plan and the end stage report and authorize the next stage;
- Decide on escalated issues and requests for advice from the project manager and approve changes and completed products;
- Direct and guide the project, communicate to stakeholders and make sure there is an effective risk management;
- Assure that acceptance criteria are met and that all specialists products are accepted;
- Confirm the acceptance of the project product, approve the end stage report and authorize the project closure;
- Authorize follow-on recommendations to be distributed to corporate, programme management or customer;
- Transfer the responsibility of the benefits management approach to corporate, programme management or customer.

B.2 Executive

The executive is ultimately responsible for the success of the project. He has to ensure tha the project is achieving its objectives and is delivering the project product, thus enabling th forecast benefits to be attained. The executive is owner of the business case.

Derived from this, the executive will:

- Design and appoint the project management team;
- Oversee the development of the project brief;
- Ensure alignment with corporate, programme management or customer;
- Oversee the development of the business case;
- Secure the funding for the project;
- Approve any supplier contract with external parties;
- Organize and chair project board meetings;
- Hold the senior user to account for realizing the benefits, and ensure that benefit reviews take place;
- Hold the senior supplier to account for the quality and integrity of the specialist approac and specialist products;
- Monitor and control the progress of the project at strategic level, in particular reviewin the business case on a regular basis;
- Ensure that issues and risks associated with the business case are identified, assessed an controlled;
- Take decisions on escalated issues and risks, with continued focus on business justification
- Escalate issues and risks to corporate, programme management or customer if projec tolerances are forecast to be exceeded;
- Transfer responsibility for post-project benefits reviews to corporate, programm management or customer.

B.3 Senior user

The senior user represents the interests of all those who will use the project product (including operations and managing maintenance services) and is therefore responsible for specifying the needs of those he represents. He specifies the benefits and is held to account by demonstrating to corporate, programme management or customer that the forecast benefits have in fact been realized.

Derived from this, the senior user will:

- Provide the customer quality expectations and acceptance criteria;
- Ensure that the outcome and the benefits are specified;
- Ensure that the products meet user requirements, that the products will deliver the desired outcome and that benefits are realized;
- Ensure that the required user resources are made available;
- Resolve user requirements and priority conflicts;
- Brief and advise user management on all project matters;
- Undertake project assurance from the user point of view;
- Decide on escalated issues with focus on safeguarding benefits;
- Provide user view on follow-on recommendations;
- Maintain business performance stability during the transition of the project product into business operations;
- Provide a statement about actual versus forecast benefits at benefits reviews.

B.4 Senior supplier

The senior supplier represents the interests of all those who design, develop, facilitate, produce, procure and implement the project product. This role is accountable for the quality of the products delivered by the supplier(s) and is responsible for the technical integrity of the project.

Derived from this, the senior supplier will:

- Assess and confirm the viability of the project's approach;
- Ensure that the proposals for designing and developing are realistic;
- Advise on selection of design, development and acceptance methods;
- Ensure quality procedures are used correctly;
- Ensure that the required supplier resources are made available;
- Resolve supplier requirements and priority conflicts;
- Brief non-technical management on supplier aspects;
- Undertake project assurance from the supplier point of view;
- Decide on escalated issues with a focus on safeguarding supplier interests.

B.5 Project manager

The project manager is responsible for the day-to-day management of the project on behalf of the project board. The project manager's prime responsibility is to ensure that the project delivers the required products within the specified tolerances and is capable of achieving th benefits defined in the business case.

Derived from this, the project manager will:

- Prepare the project brief;
- Advise the executive on the project management team;
- Create and maintain the daily and lessons log;
- Define and document the tailoring of PRINCE2;
- Establish and manage project controls and approaches;
- Create and maintain the issue and risk register;
- Prepare the PID and its components;
- Prepare project, stage and exception plans;
- Prepare and authorize work packages;
- Prepare highlight, issue, end stage, exception and end project reports;
- Liaise with project assurance and other stakeholders;
- Lead and motivate the project team and supervise the project support;
- Manage information flow between directing and delivering processes;
- Manage the production and integration of the project's products, the overall progress and the use of resources;
- Initiate corrective actions when necessary;
- Advise the project board of any deviation from the plan.

B.6 Team manager

The team manager's prime responsibility is to ensure production of the assigned products to an appropriate quality and within other tolerances agreed. The team manager takes directions from and reports to the project manager.

Derived from this, the team manager will:

- Prepare the team plan and agree the work package and the team plan with the project manager;
- Recommend on how PRINCE2 may be tailored to suit the management of work packages;
- Plan, monitor and manage the team's work;
- Liaise with project assurance and project support;
- Ensure appropriate entries are made in the quality register;

- Hand over the completed products to the project manager;
- Produce the checkpoint reports;
- Identify and advise the project manager of any issues and risks associated with the work package;
- Assist the project manager in examining issues and risks;
- Manage issues and risks assigned by the project manager;
- Deliver the completed work package to the project manager.

B.7 Project assurance

The prime responsibility of project assurance is to undertake assurance in relation to the execution and performance of the project on behalf of the individual members of the project board. This responsibility cannot be delegated to the project manager.

Derived from this, the business assurance will:

- Assist in the development of the business case and benefits management approach;
- Advise on the selection of project management team members;
- Ensure liaison between business, user and supplier;
- Advise on the risk management approach;
- Check periodically that the project remains viable and is compliant with standards from corporate, programme management or customer;
- Review the project's finances;
- Check that contractor payments are authorized;
- Verify that solutions are providing value for money;
- Ensure that issues and risks are identified and managed correctly;
- Assess that aggregate risks remains within tolerance;
- Monitor progress against plan and tolerances.

The user assurance will:

- Advise on the communication management approach and stakeholder engagement;
- Ensure that the appropriate people are involved in documenting the product descriptions, and that the specifications of users' needs are accurate, complete and unambiguous;
- Assess whether the solution will meet users' needs;
- Ensure quality activities have proper users' representation;
- Ensure that user liaison is functioning effectively;
- Advise on the impact of issues from a user perspective;
- Monitor risks to the users.

The supplier assurance will:

- Review the product descriptions;
- Advise on quality management approach and change control approach;
- Advise on the project approach and methods;
- Ensure that the supplier and operating standards are defined, met and used to goo effect;
- Ensure the scope of the project is not changed unnoticed;
- Ensure that quality control procedures are adhered to correctly;
- Advise on the impact of issues from a production perspective;
- Monitor risks associated with the production aspects of the project.

B.8 Change authority

The prime responsibility of the change authority is to approve requests for change and off specifications on behalf of the project board. The project manager could be assigned as the change authority for some aspects of the project.

Derived from this, the change authority will:

- Review and approve or reject all requests for change and off-specifications within the delegated limits of authority and change budget set by the project board;
- Refer to the project board if any delegated limits of authority or allocated change budge are forecast to be exceeded.

B.9 Project support

The responsibilities of the project support can vary depending on the project, the project manager and the project environment. The role supports the project manager and the project management team and reports to the project manager. The provision of a project support is optional.

The following is a suggested list of tasks:

- Set up and maintaining project files;
- Establish document control procedures;
- Collect actual data and forecasts;
- Update plans;
- Assist with the compilation of plans and reports;

- Administer and assist with project board meetings and quality activities;
- Maintain the quality register and archive quality records;
- Maintain logs and registers as delegated by the project manager;
- Administer change control procedures;
- Maintain configuration items records;
- Contribute expertise in using specialist tools and techniques.

Appendix C Example product-based planning

Product breakdown structure for a Conference

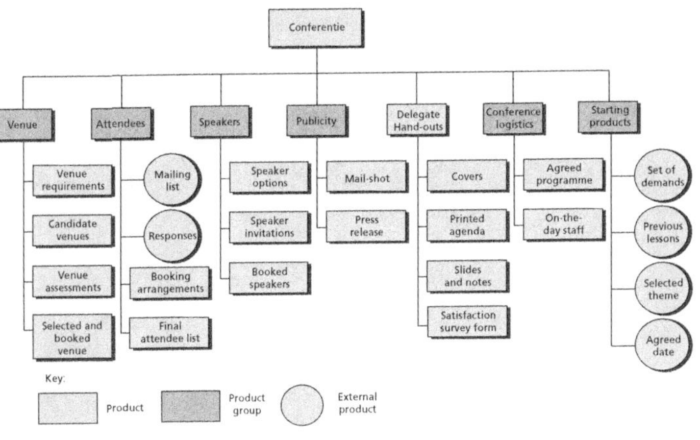

Figure. C. Example of product breakdown structure for a Conference (source: AXELOS Ltd.)

Product description of venue requirements

Table C1 Example of product description of venue requirements for a Conference

Identifier	**01**
Title	• Venue requirements
Purpose	• To identify the requirements that must be met by suitable venues for the conference
Composition	• Facilities required • Parking capacity • Attendees capacity • Accommodation capacity
Derivation	• PID, agreed date, previous lessons
Format	• Template of Purchase Department
Development skills	• Conference organizer
Quality criteria	• Specifications derived from input documents • Conditions of Purchase Department
Quality tolerance	• Quantities specified – 10%
Quality method	• Inspection of capacity • Quality review of facilities
Quality skills	• Familiar with conditions of Purchase Department • Familiar with organizing conferences
Responsibilities	• Producer: Peter. • Reviewers: Angela and William. • Approver: Head of Marketing & Sales.

Product flow diagram for a Conference

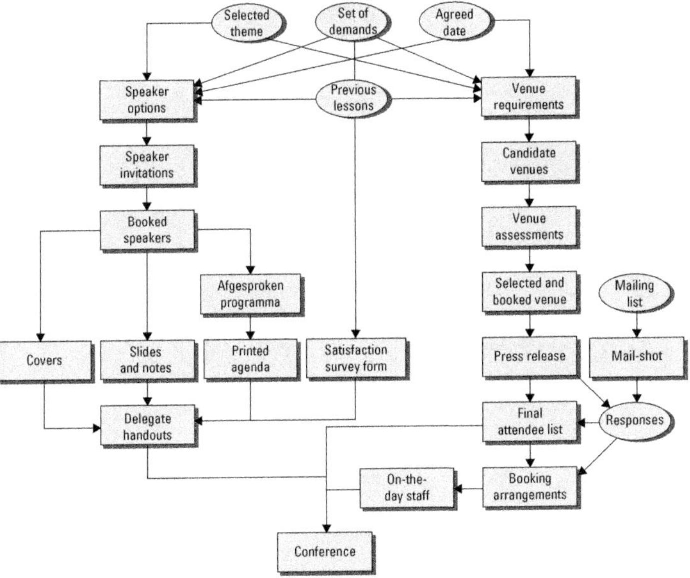

Figure. C2 Example of product flow diagram for a Conference (source: AXELOS Ltd.)

Appendix D
Glossary

Accept (risk response)	A risk response that means that the organization takes the chance that the risk will occur, with full impact on objectives if it does.
Acceptance	The formal act of acknowledging that the project has met agreed acceptance criteria and thereby met the requirements of its stakeholders.
Acceptance criteria	Measurable criteria that the project product must meet before the customer will accept it.
Accountable	Required or expected to justify actions or decisions. Accountability cannot be delegated, unlike responsibility.
Activity	A thing a person or group does. It is usually defined as part of a process or plan.
Agile and agile methods	A flexible way of working that is typified by collaboration, prioritization, iterative and incremental delivery, and timeboxing. There are several methods that are classed as agile, such as Scrum and Kanban. PRINCE2 is completely compatible with working in an agile way.
Approach	See management, delivery and project approach.
Approval	The formal confirmation that a product is complete and meets its requirements (less any concessions) as defined by its product description.
Approver	The person or group (e.g. a project board) who is authorized to approve a product as being complete and fit for purpose.
Assumption	A statement that is taken as being true for the purpose of planning.
Assurance	All the systematic actions necessary to provide confidence that the target is appropriate. See also project assurance and quality assurance.
Authority	The right to allocate resources and make decisions.
Avoid (risk response)	A risk response to a threat where the threat either can no longer have an impact or can no longer happen.
Backlog	A list of features to be realized for a product, mostly described in user stories.
Baseline	Reference levels against which an entity is monitored and controlled.
Baseline management product	A management product, when approved, is subject to change control.
Benefit	The measurable improvement resulting from an outcome perceived as an advantage by one or more stakeholders.
Benefits management approach	An approach that defines the benefits management actions and benefits reviews that must be put into place to ensure that the project's outcomes are achieved and to confirm that the project's benefits are realized.

Burn chart	A technique showing the actual work that still has to be done against the planned work to do over time and that is updated regularly.
Business case	The justification for an initiative, and against which continuing viability is tested.
Centre of excellence	A corporate function providing standards with corresponding knowledge management, assurance and training.
Change authority	A person or group to which the project board may delegate responsibility for the consideration of requests for change or off-specifications.
Change budget	The budget allocated to the change authority available to be spent on authorized requests for change.
Change control	The procedure that ensures that all changes that may affect the project's agreed objectives are identified, assessed and then approved, rejected or deferred.
Change control approach	A description of how and by whom the project's products will be controlled and protected.
Checkpoint	A team-level, time-driven review of progress.
Checkpoint report	A time-driven report from a team to the project manager on work package progress.
Closure notification	Advice from the project board to inform the host sites and the other stakeholders that the project resources and support services can be disbanded.
Closure recommendation	A recommendation prepared by the project manager for the project board to send as a project closure notification when the board is satisfied that the project can be closed.
Communication management approach	A description of the means and frequency of communication between the project and its stakeholders.
Concession	An off-specification that is accepted by the change authority without corrective action.
Configuration item	An entity that is subject to change control. The entity may be a component of a product, a product or a set of products in a release.
Configuration item record	A record that describes the status, version and variant of a configuration item, and any details of important relationships between them.
Configuration management	Technical and administrative activities concerned with the controlled change of a product.
Configuration management system	The set of processes, tools and databases that are used to manage configuration data.
Constraints	The restrictions or limitations by which the project is bound.
Contingency plan	A plan intended for use only if a risk materializes, sometimes called a fall-back plan.
Corporate, programme management or customer standards	The overarching standards to which the project must adhere.

Corrective action	A set of actions to resolve a threat to a plan's tolerances or an off-specification.
Customer	The person or group who commissioned the work and will benefit from the end results.
Customer's quality expectations	The quality expected by the customer from the project product, captured in the project product description.
Daily log	A log used to record issues that can be handled by the project manager informally.
Deliverable	See output.
Delivery approach	The specialist approach used to create the products.
Delivery step	A step within the delivery approach characterized by the techniques used, or the products created.
Dependency (plan)	A situation in which one activity can influence another activity. An internal dependency is a dependency between two project activities. An external dependency is a dependency between a project activity and a non-project activity.
Dis-benefit	A measurable decline resulting from an outcome perceived as negative by one or more stakeholders, which reduces one or more organizational objective(s).
Embedding (PRINCE2)	What an organization needs to do to adopt PRINCE2 as its corporate project management method and encourage its widespread use.
End project report	A report given by the project manager to the project board, that confirms the handover of all products and provides an updated business case and an assessment of how well the project has done against the original PID.
End stage assessment	The review by the project board of the end stage report to decide whether to approve the next stage plan.
End stage report	A report given by the project manager to the project board at the end of each intermediate management stage, providing information about the project status and the project's performance during the last management stage.
Enhance (risk response)	A risk response to an opportunity to enhance the probability of the event occurring and/or the impact of the event should it occur.
Epic	A high-level definition of a requirement. An epic will be refined and broken down into multiple sub-requirements.
Event-driven control	A control that takes place when a specific event occurs, e.g. when escalating a risk or an issue and at the end of a management stage.
Exception	A situation where it can be forecast that there will be a deviation beyond the tolerance levels agreed.
Exception assessment	A review by the project board to approve or reject an exception plan.
Exception plan	A plan to recover or avoid a forecast deviation from agreed tolerances in the stage or project plan. An exception plan often follows an exception report. An exception plan covers the remaining period of the plan it replaces.

Exception report	A description of the exception, its impact, the options and a recommendation. It is prepared by the project manager for the project board.
Executive	The single individual with overall responsibility for ensuring that a project meets its objectives and delivers the projected benefits. The executive is the chair of the project board, represents the customer and is owner for the business case.
Exploit (risk response)	A risk response to an opportunity by seizing the opportunity to ensure that it will happen and the impact will be realized.
Follow-on action recommendations	Recommended actions related to unfinished work, ongoing issues and risks, and any other activities needed to put a product into use.
Governance (corporate)	The ongoing activity of maintaining a sound system of internal control to protect assets, earning capacity and the reputation of the organization.
Governance (project)	Those areas of corporate governance that are specifically related to project activities.
Handover	The transfer of ownership of products from the supplier to the customer. There may be a phased delivery. The final handover takes place at the end of the project.
Highlight report	A time-driven report from the project manager to the project board on management stage progress.
Impact (of risk)	The (possible) effect on the achievement of the objectives if a risk materializes.
Information radiator	A wall or board containing project information that can be readily accessed by people working on the project. Among others it shows work to do, in progress and done.
Inherent risk	The exposure to a specific risk before any action has been taken to manage it.
Initiation stage	The period in which a solid foundation is established for the delivery of the project product.
Issue	Any relevant event that has happened and not was planned, and requires management action. It can be a request for change, an off-specification, or a problem or concern.
Issue register	A register used to capture and maintain information of the issues that are being managed formally.
Issue report	A report containing the description, impact assessment and recommendations for an issue being handled formally.
Key performance indicator (KPI)	A measure of performance used to help an organization define and evaluate how successful it is in making progress towards its objectives.
Lessons log	An informal repository for lessons that are useful for this project or other projects.
Lessons report	A report that documents any lessons that can be useful for other projects.

Log	An informal repository that does not require any agreement by the project board on its format, composition and use (daily log and lessons log).
Management approach	The management actions to be put into place to ensure that an aspect of project management will be dealt with effectively.
Management product	A product that will be required as part of managing the project and establishing and maintaining quality. There are three types: baselines, reports and records.
Management stage	The section of a project that the project manager is managing on behalf of the project board at any one time, at the end of which the project board will wish to decide whether to continue with the project or not.
Maturity model	A method of assessing organizational capability in a given area of skill.
Milestone	A significant event in a plan's schedule to review its progress.
Off-specification	Something that should be provided by the project, but currently is not or is forecast not to be.
Operational and maintenance acceptance	The acceptance by the person or group who will support the product after it has been handed over into the operational environment.
Outcome	The result of change, normally affecting real-world behaviour and/or circumstances.
Output	A specialist product that is or will be handed over from the supplier to the customer.
Performance targets	A plan's goals for time, cost, quality, scope, benefits and risk.
Plan	A detailed proposal for doing or achieving something which specifies the what, when, how and by whom. PRINCE2 distinguishes project plans, stage plans, team plans and exception plans.
Planned closure	The activities required to close a project.
Planning horizon	The period of time for which it is possible to plan accurately.
Portfolio	The totality of an organization's investment (or segment thereof) in the changes required to achieve its strategic objectives.
Premature closure	The activities required to close a project before its planned closure.
Prerequisites (plan)	Any fundamental aspects that must be in place, and remain in place, for a plan to succeed.
PRINCE2 principles	The guiding obligations for good project management practice that form the basis of a PRINCE2 project.
PRINCE2 project	A project that applies the PRINCE2 principles.
Probability	The evaluated likelihood of a particular risk actually happening, including a consideration of the frequency with which this may arise.
Problem/concern	An issue, not being a change request or an off-specification that the project manager needs to resolve or escalate.

Procedure	A series of activities conducted in a certain order or manner to accomplish a specific objective, including the functional responsibilities, required info and methods.
Process	A structured set of tasks designed to accomplish a specific objective (big picture). A process takes one or more defined inputs and turns them into defined outputs.
Producer	The person or group responsible for developing a product.
Product	An input or output, whether tangible or intangible, that can be described in advance, created and tested. (management products and specialist products).
Product breakdown structure	A hierarchy of all the products to be produced during a plan.
Product checklist	A list of the major products of a plan, plus key dates in their delivery.
Product description	A description of a product's purpose, composition, derivation and quality criteria. It is produced as soon as possible after the need for the product is identified.
Product flow diagram	A diagram showing the sequence in their production and the interdependencies of the products listed in a product breakdown structure.
Product status account	A report on the status of products.
Product-based planning	An approach leading to a comprehensive plan based on the creation and delivery of required outputs. The approach considers prerequisite products, quality requirements and interdependencies.
Programme	A temporary organization that is created to coordinate, direct and oversee the implementation of a set of related projects and activities in order to deliver outcomes and benefits related to the organization's strategic objectives.
Project	A temporary organization that is created for the purpose of delivering one or more business products according to an agreed business case.
Project approach	A description of the way in which the work of the project is to be delivered.
Project assurance	The project board's responsibilities to assure itself that the project is being conducted correctly. PRINCE2 distinguishes business, user and supplier assurance.
Project authorization notification	Advice form the project board to inform the host sites and other stakeholders that the project has been authorized and to request any necessary logistical support sufficient for the duration of the project.
Project brief	A description of the purpose, cost, time and performance requirements, and constraints for a project. The project brief is created in the starting up a project.
Project closure notification	Advice from the project board to inform the host sites and other stakeholders that the project resources and support services can be disbanded. It should also indicate a closure date for costs to be charged to the project.

Project initiation documentation A set of documents that brings together the key information needed to start the project on a sound basis and that conveys the information to all concerned with the project.

Project initiation notification Advice from the project board to inform the host sites and other stakeholders that the project is being initiated and to request any necessary logistical support, sufficient for the initiation stage.

Project lifecycle The period from the project's initiation to the acceptance of the project product.

Project management The planning, delegating, monitoring and control of all aspects of the project, and the motivation of those involved, to achieve the project objectives within the expected performance targets for time, cost, quality, scope, benefits and risk.

Project management team The people assigned to the project board, project manager, team managers, project assurance and project support roles.

Project management team structure The structure of the project management team roles, and their delegation and reporting relationships.

Project manager The person given the authority and responsibility to manage the project on a day-to-day basis to deliver the required products within the constraints agreed on with the project board.

Project mandate An external product generated by the authority commissioning the project that forms the trigger for starting up a project.

Project office A temporary office set up to support the execution of a project. If used, the project office undertakes the responsibility of the project support role.

Project plan A high-level plan showing the major products of the project, when they will be delivered and at what cost, used by the project board to monitor progress.

Project product What the project must deliver in order to gain acceptance.

Project product description The product description of the project product to gain agreement from the user on the project's output and requirements.

Project support An administrative role in the project management team. Project support can be in the form of advice or help with tools and administration services such as filing and the collection of actual data.

Proximity (of risk) The time factor of risk i.e. when the risk may occur. The impact of a risk may vary depending on when the risk occurs.

Quality The degree to which a set of inherent characteristics of a product or system fulfils requirements, needs and expectations that are stated, self-evident or mandatory.

Quality assurance A planned and systematic process that provides confidence that outputs will match quality criteria when tested under quality control.

Quality control The process of monitoring specific project results to determine whether they comply with relevant standards and of identifying ways to eliminate causes of unsatisfactory performance.

Quality criteria A description of the quality specification that the product must meet, and the quality measurements that will be applied by those inspecting the finished product.

Quality inspection A systematic, structured assessment of a product carried out by one or more specialists to determine whether the product complies with the specifications.

Quality management The coordinated activities to direct and control an organization with regard to quality.

Quality management approach An approach defining the quality techniques and standards to be applied, and the various responsibilities for achieving the required quality levels, during a project.

Quality management system The complete set of quality standards, procedures and responsibilities for an organization or specific entity within that organization.

Quality records Evidence kept to demonstrate that the required quality assurance and quality control activities have been carried out.

Quality register A register containing summary details of all planned and completed quality activities.

Quality review A systematic, structured assessment of a product carried out by a team in a planned, documented and organized fashion.

Quality review technique A technique with defined roles and a specific structure, designed to assess whether a product in the form of a document (or similar) is complete, adheres to standards and meets its agreed quality criteria.

Records Dynamic management products that maintain information regarding project progress.

Reduce (risk response) A proactive action to reduce the probability of a risk and/or reduce the impact of the risk, should it occur.

Register A formal repository that requires agreement by the project board on its format, composition and use. (issue, quality and risk register).

Release The set of products in a phased handover.

Report A management product providing a snapshot of the status on certain aspects of the project.

Request for change A proposal for a change to a baseline (one of the three types of issue).

Residual risk The risk remaining after the risk response has been applied.

Responsible Having the obligation to do something, or having control over or care for someone, as part of one's job or role. A responsibility can be delegated, unlike accountability.

Responsible authority The person or group commissioning the project (typically the corporate, programme management or customer) who has the authority to commit resources and funds on behalf of the commissioning organization.

Reviewer A person or group independent of the producer who assesses whether a product meets its requirements as defined in its product description.

Risk An uncertain event or set of events that, should it occur, will have an effect on the achievement of objectives.

Risk actionee A person responsible for carrying out a risk response in case a risk owner cannot carry out the risk response himself. The risk actionee reports to the risk owner.

Risk appetite An organization's attitude towards risk-taking that dictates the amount of risk that it considers acceptable.

Risk estimation The estimation of probability and impact of an individual risk.

Risk evaluation The process of understanding the net effect of the identified threats and opportunities on an activity when aggregated together.

Risk exposure The extent of risk present in the organization at the time.

Risk management The systematic application of principles, approaches and processes to the tasks of identifying and assessing risks, planning and implementing risk responses and communicating risk management activities with stakeholders.

Risk management approach An approach describing the goals of applying risk management, as well as the procedure that will be adopted, roles and responsibilities, risk tolerances, the timing of risk management interventions, the tools and techniques that will be used, and the reporting requirements.

Risk owner A named individual who is responsible for the management, monitoring and control of all aspects of a particular risk assigned to them, including the implementation of the selected responses to address the threats or maximize the opportunities.

Risk profile A description of probability and possible impact of a risk.

Risk register A record of identified risks relating to an initiative, including their status and history.

Risk response Action that may be taken to bring a situation to a level where exposure to risk is acceptable to the organization.

Risk response category A category of risk response. Possible risk responses are avoid and reduce (threat), exploit and enhance (opportunity), and further transfer, share, accept and prepare contingency plans for threats as well as opportunities.

Risk tolerance line A line on the summary risk profile that distinguishes risks that do not need to be referred to the project board and risks that have to be referred to the project board.

Scope The total of the products to be delivered and the extent of their requirements. It is described by the plan's product breakdown structure and product descriptions.

Scrum A specific agile method to product delivery, developed by Ken Schwaber and Jeff Sutherland.

Scrum master A Scrum role that is responsible for ensuring Scrum is understood and enacted and that the Scrum team adheres to Scrum theory, practice and rules.

Senior supplier — The project board role accountable for delivering the project product on time, within budget and conform specifications and responsible for the technical integrity of the project.

Senior user — The project board role accountable for ensuring that user needs are specified correctly and that the solution meets those needs.

Share (risk response) — A risk response to either a threat or an opportunity through the application of a pain/gain formula.

Specialist product — A product whose development is the subject of the plan. The specialist products – also known as deliverables – are specific to an individual project. See also output.

Sponsor — The main driving force behind a programme or project. The sponsor is usually the executive in the project or the person appointing the executive.

Sprint — A fixed timeframe (2-4 weeks) for creating selected features from the backlog.

Stage — See management stage.

Stage plan — A detailed plan used as the basis for project management control throughout a management stage.

Stakeholder — Any individual, group or organization that can affect, be affected by, or perceive itself to be affected by an initiative.

Start-up — The pre-project activities undertaken by the executive and the project manager to produce the outline business case, project brief and initiation stage plan.

Supplier — The person, group or groups responsible for the supply of the project's specialist products.

Tailoring — Adapting a method or process to suit the situation in which it will be used.

Team manager — The person responsible for the production of products allocated by the project manager as defined in a work package.

Team plan — An optional level of plan used as a basis for team management control when executing work packages.

Theme — An aspect of project management that continually needs be addressed, and that requires specific treatment for the PRINCE2 processes to be effective.

Threat — An uncertain event that could have a negative impact on objectives or benefits.

Time schedule — A schematic representation of a time schedule, in which the duration of activities is shown positioned along a time bar.

Time-driven control — A management control that is periodic in nature (e.g. every two weeks), to enable the next higher authority to monitor progress (highlight report and checkpoint report).

Timebox A finite period of time to achieve a goal or to meet an objective without the possibility of shifting the deadline. Timeboxes can be at various levels (sprint, stage and project).

Tolerance The permissible deviation above and below a plan's target (e.g. for time, cost, scope, quality, benefits and risk) without the need to escalate the deviation to the next level of management. Tolerances are applied at project, stage and team levels.

Transfer (risk response) A response to a threat where a third party takes on responsibility for some of the financial impact of the threat.

Transformation A distinct change to the way an organization conducts all or part of its business.

Trigger An event or decision that triggers a process to start.

User The person or group who will use the project product.

User acceptance The acceptance by the person or group who will use the product after it has been handed over into the operational environment.

User story A description of a feature in the form of who wants or needs what and why.

Variant A variation of a baselined product (e.g. this pocket guide has an English, German, French and Dutch variant).

Version A specific baseline of a product, usually with conventions that enable the sequence or date of the baseline to be identified.

Waterfall method A development approach that is linear and sequential with distinct goals for each delivery stage (e.g. design, build, test and implementation).

Work package The set of information relevant to the creation of one or more products.

About the authors

Bert Hedeman is P3M3 consultant and partner of HWP Consulting BV. He has more than 35 years' experience in project, program and portfolio management, of which 12 years at an international construction company and some years at an international engineering company. Bert is also coach and accredited trainer for PRINCE2, PRINCE2 Agile, AgilePM, MSP, P3O, MoP, M_o_R, and IPMA. Bert is co-author of several books e.g. 'Project Management based on PRINCE2' and 'Managing of Agile projects'. Furthermore Bert is assistant professor at the master of Project Management at the University of Applied Science Utrecht.

Ron Seegers is a senior project management trainer and coach at Projectmeester. Ron is an accredited trainer in PRINCE2, AgilePM and PRINCE2 Agile, and is co-author of 'Managing of Agile projects'. For organizations to have better results, Ron inspires them to adopt and adapt the aforementioned methods and frameworks, like Scrum. Ron has been active in project management since the mid 90's in roles as project manager, manager of project managers, consultant, trainer and coach.

Printed in Great Britain
by Amazon

20738482R00099